AF413320

Upon the Altar of Freedom

Upon the Altar of Freedom

From Blue Star Family to Silver Star and Beyond

JILL SMITH, TERRY SMITH, *and* RICHARD SALCIDO

Foreword by Byron Edwards

RESOURCE *Publications* · Eugene, Oregon

To all the military veterans and their families who have ever placed a
sacrifice upon the altar of freedom over the past 247 years, that this
nation of God-given liberties shall not perish from the earth.

Contents

Foreword

If you hail from a military family, you will read *Upon the Altar of Freedom* with deep appreciation. You will nod your head in acknowledgement of similar situations you have personally experienced.

If like me, you are from a non-military family, I strongly encourage you to read this story, for you will learn much about the true depth of suffering and sacrifice required to maintain freedom. I assure you; you will be glad that you did. This book tells the life of an extremely talented individual, Jeremy Smith, gifted with an unselfish nature and characteristics of genuine friendship, leadership, and love. He used these traits in service to America as a soldier in the U.S. Army, where he achieved extraordinary success both in combat and in peace. His family has a long and proud military tradition, which he certainly upheld.

Jeremy's story will open your eyes, your heart, and your tear ducts. You will cry. Butterflies will bring tears to your eyes. One of the groomsmen at my wedding, my best friend, served as a captain in the U.S. Army in Vietnam. He lost his brother, also an Army captain, in that war. I thought I understood his pain. After reading *Upon the Altar of Freedom*, I realized I did not. The emotional scars that combat veterans have are not always apparent because they often hide those wounds. They don't want to "burden" family and friends with them, talk about them, or seek help for them.

Jeremy Smith suffered as a young man. He loved his family and was a Christian and a true friend, a real brother to his army colleagues. Pursuant to his sacrifice, his story can continue to enlighten and help many, many others.

Byron Edwards, PhD, Author
Vice President for Academic Affairs, Nossi College of Art
Nashville, Tennessee
November 2020

Preface

In 2018, I observed a solemn ceremony in Kentucky honoring a combat veteran who fought in Iraq and Afghanistan during the war on terror. I sat in amazement noting about seventy of his combat buddies who dropped everything on a moment's notice, spent hundreds and in some cases thousands of dollars travelling, and somberly participated in this event recognizing one of our nation's unsung heroes. The venerable veteran was Jeremy Doyle Smith, an Army sergeant who touched the lives of his comrades so deeply that it compelled them to attend. Some had served with him fifteen years ago, and one came all the way from Alaska. Intrigued and incredulously impressed, I wanted to discover and share his life's story. Later that month, I approached his parents, Terry and Jill Smith, and asked them if they would like to tell their son's story in a book. Having never done such an endeavor before, they eagerly yet apprehensively embraced the notion, knowing that it would take an emotional toll on them. However, they wanted to honor the life of Jeremy in a way that might help other veterans and their families.

Terry and Jill reached out to many of Jeremy's brothers-in-arms about this undertaking. All of them, without fail, applauded the effort and gave their enthusiastic support. However, only a fraction could open up and talk about their encounters in combat and with Sergeant Smith. The others, although they deeply wanted to, found this burden too heavy emotionally. At first, I feared that we wouldn't get enough content to do justice for telling Jeremy's story. Some tried but simply couldn't follow through with it because the pain ran too deep. Others simply couldn't begin to talk about it at all. As this venture moved along, however, a sufficient number of courageous souls mustered the strength to share their experiences in order to honor their revered comrade. During most of the interviews, the combat veteran with whom I spoke teared up to one degree or another.

Terry and Jill also reached out to family and friends. As a result, a torrent of input steadily flowed in from them throughout the opening months of this literary journey. The outpouring of exceptional love for Jeremy from his family and friends impressed and amazed me. One thing became indisputably apparent. Even though he loomed larger than life, Jeremy deeply touched the lives of others with genuine love, putting their interests ahead of his own.

Although a heavy burden, Terry and Jill spoke with me candidly about the life of their son, as did Leah their daughter. I spent numerous bittersweet moments with them as they recounted Jeremy's life. Joy and love beamed from their eyes while a wavering voice tried to subdue the sorrow. At times, they simply couldn't restrain the tears. Unless a person had suffered such things, we could only pretend to understand. Such feelings couldn't be comprehended but only experienced personally. How daunting the turmoil that Terry and Jill felt within as they retold Jeremy's life story and reviewed the draft chapters of the book. Terry and Jill Smith proved themselves selfless and morally courageous by enduring such pain in the hopes of helping others.

As I dove into this project, I acquired a deeper understanding for the true depth of suffering and sacrifice that combat veterans and their families endure for the sake of freedom and liberty, our freedom and liberty. One of the service members whom I interviewed explained it thus, "The service of many combat veterans is like a person running into a burning house to save the lives of other people. In the process, the hero endures third degree burns and lives out the rest of his life scarred and disfigured. The hero isn't happy about these permanent lifelong injuries, his life significantly altered forever. However, if someone asked him if he would do it all over again, without hesitation, the answer will always be unequivocally *Yes!*" Combat veterans don't simply sacrifice for a season with the trials and tribulations lasting only while in the combat zone or theater of war. They bring the battlefield home within them, while leaving part of their soul on that hallowed ground where they fought and bled alongside their comrades-in-arms.

A medic holds a dying soldier in his arms knowing he can do nothing for him. He comforts his friend during the final moments of breath as he sees the light of life fade from the wounded soldier's eyes. Such experiences permanently dwell deep within our combat veterans. These veterans can only hope to eventually learn how to manage this pain but will never be entirely free from such. They carry the scars of battle with them emotionally for the rest of their lives. Consequently, most combat veterans suffer post-traumatic stress disorder (PTSD) to one degree or another, be it nightmares or agitation in response to a loud noise. Many only suffer mild symptoms. However, possibly as high as 20 percent of combat veterans suffer this condition significantly. Most hesitate to get help because they don't want to admit that they have a disorder. The stigma of such a malady prevails not only in society but also in the military itself. As long as it does, hurting veterans will hide in the shadows rather than come forward for help. On average, an estimated seventeen to twenty-two veteran suicides occur each day in a desperate attempt to end the torment.

Medical research has revealed that traumatic events alter brain functions to create an overactive amygdala and an underactive prefrontal cortex. Consequently, those with PTSD suffer from nightmares, flashbacks, emotional flooding, reactive anger, excessive negative emotions, and hypervigilance. Continual stress can release hormones in a manner and volume that damage the brain cells of the hippocampus. As a result, the brain has difficulty filing away traumatic memories which then tend to constantly replay in the mind of the afflicted person. These studies also suggest that those born with a smaller hippocampus may be more susceptible to PTSD. Therefore, we shouldn't view this disorder as mental, emotional, or moral weakness. It occurs as a result of genetic brain characteristics or from cerebral damage. Subsequently, society shouldn't view PTSD as a stigma. We do a good job mending our veterans who sustain physical wounds. Now we need to do the same for those who suffer emotional/mental wounds.

Because of PTSD, the lives of many combat veterans and their families change forever, a bane for which none of them opted yet is the high price demanded for a nation to have freedom and liberty. Therefore, the next time you go out for ice cream on a Saturday afternoon with a loved one, remember these sufferings and sacrifices. The next time you go to a Tuesday evening soccer game to watch your children play, remember that combat veterans secured that freedom for you. The next time you travel on a weekend excursion, remember that a military family will forevermore suffer grief to afford you this blessing. Most of all, never forget that the combat veteran would serve and suffer all over again for you if required of them.

Researching for this manuscript and interviewing these valiant veterans enhanced my personal awareness and appreciation for what they and their families go through for the sake of our freedoms and liberties. Having served in the Army for twelve years myself, I thought that I had a high level of gratitude for such veterans and their sacrifices. After writing this book, I realized that my gratefulness barely scratched the surface of what they deserved yet would never demand from us. A family forevermore would deal with hypervigilance and irrational emotions within the household because their loved one served in combat. A wife would stand helplessly in the dark of night as her husband thrashed on the floor in the horrible grip of a nightmare.

The impact of these events often lasts a lifetime and are endured so that you and I can enjoy a myriad of liberties and blessings, most of which we take for granted. *Upon the Altar of Freedom* is the life story of one such combat veteran and his family. Their depth of patriotism and love for the United States of America is also rivaled by the grief and suffering required to retain the former. Although this is a biography, chapter 1 unfolds as historical fiction based on the types of nightmares and torments that Sergeant Jeremy Smith endured. Since he rarely went into detail about them with anyone, we speculated the specifics of this chapter to illustrate an episode of the darkness of PTSD. As you read through the book, always remember this one profound truth: they embrace suffering so we can enjoy freedom.

Acknowledgments

I WISH TO PERSONALLY extend heartfelt gratitude to Terry and Jill Smith, as well as to their daughter, Leah, for enduring emotional turmoil in order to share Jeremy's life so that his story could be put down on pages. Thank you for baring your souls despite the anguish to do so. Who could know the incomprehensible agony of such a feat unless one has personally gone through the experience? It has been my distinct privilege and honor to work with you on this endeavor.

Terry, Jill, and I would like to thank each family member and friend who shared with us their experiences with Jeremy. Taking the time and effort that you did demonstrates the genuine love that you have for him, as well as the significant impact he made on your life. The telling of Jeremy's life story would have been incomplete without your input. Your participation has significantly enhanced the quality of this book.

We would also like to heartily thank all the military combat veterans who mustered the strength to talk about Jeremy and their experiences in combat. We can only ponder how difficult this was for you since most combat veterans won't discuss these matters because the emotional pain runs deep. We extend a special thanks to Sergeant Jordan Stransky and Sergeant First Class Nick Smith for taking the lead on speaking to us. This action opened the door for others to walk through. We also sincerely thank Staff Sergeant Russell Laws for his interview and for also motivating several other veterans to speak with us about Jeremy's Iraq deployment. From the bottom of our hearts, we thank all of you and appreciate your lifelong sacrifices for our freedom and liberty. We owe you a debt which we can't repay.

Abbreviations

1LT	First Lieutenant
1SG	First Sergeant
AAR	After Action Review
APC	Armored Personnel Carrier
COP	Combat Outpost
CPT	Captain
CSH	Combat Support Hospital
CSM	Command Sergeant Major
EOD	Explosive Ordinance Disposal
FOB	Forward Operating Base
IED	Improvised Explosive Device
JROTC	Junior Reserve Officers' Training Corps
Klicks	Kilometers
MOS	Military Occupational Skill
MRAP	Mine Resistant Ambush Protected
MRE	Meal Ready-to-eat
NCO	Noncommissioned Officer
OPFOR	Opposition Forces
PFC	Private First Class
PID	Positive Identification
PT	Physical Training
PTSD	Post Traumatic Stress Disorder

QRF	Quick Reaction Force
RCP	Route Clearance Patrol
ROTC	Reserve Officers' Training Corps
RPG	Rocket Propelled Grenade
SFC	Sergeant First Class
SGT	Sergeant
SPC	Specialist
SSG	Staff Sergeant
TBI	Traumatic Brain Injury
TC	Truck Commander
TOC	Tactical Operations Center
UFC	Ultimate Fighting Championship
USO	United Service Organizations
VA	Veterans Administration

I

Drowning in the Dark Place

SITTING IN HIS DIMLY lit room on a steamy August afternoon, Jeremy Smith labored to work on a Ruger Alaskan .44 Magnum pistol. Scrunching his forehead due to intense concentration, he struggled to steady his jittery hands as he meticulously filed down the sear to create smoother trigger performance. Holding the piece under a desk lamp, he strained to focus on the task at hand. He felt excessively heavy and bloated since his days as a sergeant (SGT) in the Army, having gained one hundred fifty pounds since his combat injury. He used to be in such great shape during his time in the 101st Airborne Division. He proudly served his country and had no regrets about it. The nerve-damage pain of his wounded leg caused excruciating agony when he worked out, although he pushed himself through it anyway. Accustomed to achieving high standards in all his endeavors, he didn't feel worthy of the light, so he kept his bedroom curtains closed. Demoralized by his inability to continue serving in the Army and upset that he survived combat while others didn't, anger raged within him because he could no longer fight on the battlefield to protect his country and his fellow warriors. Constantly on edge, he sometimes found solace in his murky room, the fewer stimuli the better for a mind continually on overload.

Jeremy didn't go out that day. In fact, he hadn't gone out in public much lately because he profoundly felt unsafe, unforgivable, and undeserving of love. He reasoned with himself against these irrational feelings, striving to believe that a brighter future lay ahead, that things would go back to a time when his life was happy and carefree. As a young man, he didn't realize the unending offerings upon the altar of freedom, the continual sacrifice and suffering, required to sustain liberty and blessings for the people of his nation. Although well acquainted with them now, he still immensely loved his God-given country, his family, friends, and community. So much so, he would do it all over again if needed. His life wasn't supposed to unfold this way, however. He served ten years in the Army, did three combat tours, earned medals, and successfully accomplished a myriad of missions for the United States. Consequently, he now sat alone in the grim chamber of his room, his soul as bleak as the abode in which he sat.

Jeremy felt darkness pressing in on him again, as it did numerous times before. He could tell when the torment began to encroach. He then busied himself with hours of watching television shows, watching videos about guns and cars, or playing video games. As long as he occupied his mind, it sometimes kept the darkness at bay. This evening, he intensely worked away on the pistol. Regardless, the darkness entered his room like a sinister shadow that he could only feel but never see. Despite concentrating on repairing the gun, rampant thoughts of his time in Afghanistan and Iraq intruded upon his mind. They came in as a merciless flood; cold, torrential, and unstoppable, swamping every crevasse of his psyche, often times playing out through a distorted lens of reality. He saw the faces of Afghan children flashing in his mind's eye, children smiling, laughing, and playing. He adored the little children and enjoyed the community assignments that he did to foster positive relations with the Afghan people. Their reflective smiles and laughter didn't bring Jeremy any joy, unfortunately, for he knew where this mental excursion headed. It dragged him there a multitude of times before despite his objections. He didn't want to go there now. However, at times, he couldn't stop it.

Soon, the four walls of his room faded into the Afghan countryside, as Jeremy found himself riding shotgun in a Humvee, as it cautiously navigated the streets of a village. Mud houses lined the bumpy dirt thoroughfare riddled with potholes and washed-out in spots due to rain. Most of the houses possessed a courtyard and tall mud walls for security. He saw a little Afghan girl about the age of six standing to the side of the road in front of a house. He smiled and waved to her. She smiled and waved back. Jeremy and his driver made their way to the northeast edge of the village to assess the terrain and see if the installation of culverts might facilitate good drainage and irrigation for this rural community.

Upon completing the survey, they vigilantly drove back through the village, ever watchful for improvised explosive devices (IEDs) buried in the road. When they approached the house where the little girl stood, Jeremy saw a crumpled, contorted figure lay at the mouth of the doorway to the courtyard. As they passed by, the figure looked up at them. Suddenly, outrage pierced Jeremy's heart like a dagger plunging deep within his chest. The adorable little girl who smiled at him earlier now lay in the dirt battered, bloodied, and broken, having been pummeled for waving to the Americans. Far too often, the Taliban manipulated the general populous with fear, motivating adults to severely beat children for showing support to the *foreign intruders.*

In his mind's eye, Jeremy saw the angry, distorted face of the little Afghan girl glaring at him in pain and suffering. The words *Where is the justice, American soldier?* echoed off the walls of his psyche. A deep sense of devastation engulfed him as anger and frustration taunted his shattered soul. He felt helpless to stop the epidemic of child abuse that ravaged these lands. *Something has to be done to end this monumental wrong!* repeatedly ran unchecked through his spinning mind. Powerless to do anything to protect these children from this travesty, Jeremy let out a wrathful howl jolting himself back to reality somewhat.

Drenched in sweat with his heart pounding feverishly, he recognized his dismal room and stood up forcefully, knocking his chair to the floor. Stomping his way across the carpet to a backpack that held his sacred things, he furiously tore through its contents until he found a bottle of Wild Turkey 101 Bourbon whiskey. He then guzzled and gulped down a good portion of the smooth, fiery liquid in an anxious attempt to self-medicate the anguish away. Alcohol dulled the effects of PTSD. Not wanting to become addicted to the medication that the Army and the Veterans Administration (VA) prescribed as his cure, he drank alcohol instead—in great quantities. He drank to forget the horrors that he had seen and to stop the nightmares. He could sleep if inebriated. When sober, he dreaded slumber because the nightmares prevailed. Alcohol allowed him not to dream and not to feel.

Instead of relief this time, however, Jeremy sensed the sinister shadow of torment surge with energy and power as it engulfed him in a cocoon of desolation. Despite feeling overwhelmed, he fought back arduously against this nemesis. He tried to convince himself that he lay safely in his room in Kentucky but to no avail. Intrusive thoughts continued to flood the cavern of his mind. He shook uncontrollably as the torment catapulted him again to the battlefields of Afghanistan. As he looked about, he saw that he lay prone holding a spotting scope on a rise overlooking a village, while the dry dusty heat taunted his nose and throat as he breathed. Taliban insurgency had recently increased in that area, making military operations more hazardous. He and the sniper next to him looked through their scopes for any enemy presence as an American platoon maneuvered through the village.

Scanning a row of houses that sat on a hillside above the platoon, Jeremy spotted some kind of activity in an alleyway. Taking a closer look, he saw a grown man violating a young boy about the age of ten. Jeremy lay there frozen in shock, his mind ceasing to process any thoughts due to the immense disbelief that consumed him. Finally, he sputtered in a low but alarmed voice, "Hey, do you see that? Third row of houses from the top of the hill, alleyway between the fifth and sixth houses from the left, about our eleven o'clock at five hundred meters."

Expecting to see enemy activity, the sniper gawked in skepticism, refusing to believe what his eyes saw. "No way!" he exclaimed in a whisper.

"Blow that creep's head off!" Jeremy demanded.

The sniper replied, "No, can't do it, rules of engagement."

"Fine, I'll do it myself!" Jeremy retorted shouldering his rifle in the prone position and taking careful aim.

"Don't do it, SGT," the sniper admonished. "You'll get busted."

Gently applying pressure to the trigger to ensure an accurate round downrange, Jeremy countered, "I don't care! What he's doing is wrong! It's sick!"

"They'll hang you at Leavenworth," the frustrated sniper reprimanded. Finally, in desperation, the sniper insisted, "Stand down, SGT Smith, right now! That's an order!"

As the junior noncommissioned officer (NCO) between them, Jeremy reluctantly relented, letting out a chorus of profanity. He picked his spotting scope back up and looked through it. To his horror, it appeared that the little boy looked right at him. Jeremy could seemingly hear him plead in desperation, "Why won't you do anything? What kind of person are you?" With a tortured, contorted expression on his face, the little boy glowered at Jeremy eye to eye.

In a drunken stupor, Jeremy gained some cognizance, finding himself floundering on the floor of his room, repeatedly saying, "I did nothing to help. Why didn't I do something?" Having lived by a high moral code, he condemned himself as a bad person. He then guzzled down more of the whiskey, on which he became so reliant. Once again, the sinister shadow of guilt and condemnation made its prowess known by hurling Jeremy against his will back to the days of his deployment in Iraq. He found himself manning a 50-caliber machine gun mounted atop a Stryker armored fighting vehicle at a check point along a thoroughfare. He chose this task so that he could watch over and protect his dismounted and exposed comrades manning the check point on the ground. Whenever the American troops left the wire and ventured outside their base, the Iraqi insurgents kept them under constant surveillance looking for an opportunity to strike. This put the Americans constantly on edge.

The desert sun pulsated wave after wave of dry heat down upon the soldiers, making the sixty pounds of battle armor and gear that they wore feel twice as heavy. The one-hundred-twenty-degree temperature baked

Jeremy as he stood at the ready in an armored personnel carrier (APC) that felt more like an oven than a vehicle. Drenched with perspiration, sweat seeped down his forehead and into his eyes aggravating them with a burning sensation. The desert wind blew torrid dust all around irritating his nose and parched throat. The day sluggishly dragged on hotly and heavily. Off in the distance, a sign informed the motorists that a checkpoint lay ahead, instructing them to slow down and prepare to stop. A few Iraqi police monitored traffic near the sign. Strands of concertina wire and orange cones funneled traffic into a choke point for inspection.

Suddenly, commotion in the distance shattered the broiling boredom of the scorching day. Iraqi police desperately waved their arms and yelled at a car to slow down. However, the rogue vehicle only sped up as it accelerated toward the American soldiers. As the vehicle past the trigger line, a few of the dismounted soldiers fired warning shots. The driver refused to submit, propelling his car ever closer to the American position. Sensing that his comrades stood in the way of impending peril, Jeremy opened up with the 50-caliber machine gun hurling a hail of bullets at the rogue vehicle. He determined in his heart that he would do everything in his power to stop the charging car and protect his brothers. The time that he already spent in Iraq forged him into a formidable warrior. He proved himself good at soldiering, completing his missions, and neutralizing the enemy. Performing his duties well and killing the enemy gave him a profound sense of satisfaction.

Jeremy fired his weapon true to its mark and disabled the vehicle. He felt a great sense of pride and gratification having protected his fellow soldiers against evil. A moment later the dismounted troops with weapons at the ready slowly approached the car and ordered the occupants to get out. A man and woman hysterically shrieked in grief-stricken terror as they exited the vehicle with hands raised. A few children exited the backseat crying uncontrollably. The soldiers searched the occupants and the car for weapons and explosives but found none. At that juncture, the vehicle only contained a young girl about the age of four dead in the backseat, her life snuffed out instantly by a 50-caliber round. When Jeremy got the news, he plunged deeply into despair. He was there to kill radical extremists not little children. Why didn't the vehicle stop? Why did it accelerate toward the checkpoint? An illiterate Iraqi family occupied the car. They could neither read nor understand the sign announcing the forthcoming checkpoint. The commotion of the Iraqi police only scared the driver who sped up in response. Language and cultural barriers caused regrettable confusion. As a result, tragedy ensued.

Jeremy slowly faded into black obscurity in the midst of his bedroom within his Kentucky home, repeatedly pronouncing judgment upon himself,

"I'm a monster. I don't deserve forgiveness. How could God love me?" The face of the little Iraqi girl scowled at him relentlessly demanding, "Why did you kill me? I had my whole life in front of me! What kind of person are you?" Jeremy responded only with self-condemnation as he uttered, "I'm a monster; God can't love me." If he had blacked out at this point, it would have been a blessing, but instead the town of Mosul emerged. Lately, al-Qaeda in Iraq started using female suicide bombers to wreak havoc among Iraqi society to thwart the success of the new government. For this task, the jihadists chose women emotionally vulnerable and easily exploited, whom they generally considered expendable. While manning a checkpoint guarding the center of Mosul, Jeremy's squad received a notice to be on the lookout for a suspected female suicide bomber that managed to get past two outer checkpoints on her way to the city square. Women could get through checkpoints more easily than men because of the chivalrous nature of American soldiers.

The leader of their security detail briefed them, "A female Iraqi national is suspected of carrying a bomb in her handbag. It looks like a carpetbag, green and purple in color about two feet long by one and a half high with leather straps. The suspect may also have an IED strapped to her body beneath her robe. She is believed to be in her early twenties wearing a black burka revealing only her eyes. Suspect is about five and a half feet tall weighing about one hundred twenty pounds. If she fails to comply with orders, shoot to kill."

A soldier quipped, "Full black burka, average height, average build. That narrows it down to about 50 percent of the Iraqi women!"

Jeremy smirked as he heard the soldier's remark but took the bulletin to heart. A female suicide bomber blew up the marketplace earlier in the week killing Iraqi police, as well as bystanders in an attempt to instill a lack of confidence into the people toward the new government. As the day wore on, Jeremy and his comrades inspected what seemed like a million people and vehicles as the scorching heat of the desert sun beat down upon them. Suddenly, commotion erupted about thirty meters from where Jeremy stood. An Iraqi female fitting the description of the suspected bomber broke out of line yelling, "Allahu Akbar!" She raced toward the American soldiers carrying a large handbag in her left hand and raising her right hand which appeared to be holding something. The leader of the security patrol there at the checkpoint yelled, "Shoot to kill, now!"

Jeremy quickly raised his M4 rifle and fired a three-round burst at the woman's head. Consequently, she fell lifelessly to the ground with a loud thump. Her blank still eyes devoid of life stared directly into Jeremy's, as the lifeless expression on her mutilated face permanently seared itself into his psyche. A few sappers slowly approached the woman and examined what she had in her hand, while the other soldiers ordered the Iraqi populous to evacuate the area. The sappers discovered that she simply held a black piece of plastic in her palm. The large handbag that she wielded contained no explosives, and neither did she bear any under her robe. Haunted by the woman's look of demise, Jeremy closed his eyes in deep despair. Situations like this tortured him. They forced this peaceful, fun-loving young man to be a ruthless warrior relentless against the enemy. He hated these deplorable circumstances that the enemy created. At that point, he desperately wanted to be anywhere but there.

Suddenly a loud blast exploded behind the checkpoint in the town square. The woman posed as a diversionary decoy, while the real bomber slipped past the soldiers unnoticed in the commotion. The force of the blast hurled Jeremy forward off his feet. He hit the dusty ground with a loud thwack. Choking on the hot dust, he looked up to find himself in an unfamiliar alley across town. He peered about frantically assessing his dire situation, not an American soldier in sight. There he knelt vacillating and isolated in a strange part of town. Before he could fully surmise his situation, a wisp of dirt whisked up at him as a bullet ricocheted off the ground. At that moment, Jeremy made a quick decision, no need to deliberate on what to do. He ran, determined to find an adequate fighting position from which to neutralize his assailant. Looking behind him periodically, he saw no one. In fact, he rambled through eerily empty streets and alleys as bullets recoiled off buildings and the hard dirt road around him. One struck him in the leg causing him to stumble. Jeremy immediately got up and attempted to sprint as hard as he could. However, his legs felt like heavy lead as he labored exhaustively to escape from his nemesis. While a massive jolt of pain bolted up his wounded limb with each step, an immense dread of impending demise almost paralyzed him.

Jeremy dove behind a mud-brick wall about four feet high. Struggling to catch his breath, he anxiously wrestled with a tourniquet in an attempt to place it on his wounded leg. No matter how hard he tried, he just couldn't seem to place it properly and tighten it. Sudden angst gripped him as three ricocheting rounds informed him that he was out of time and had to seek better cover. Looking back at times as he toiled through the deserted streets within an unending labyrinth of mud buildings, he could only get a glimpse every now and then of a shadowy figure relentlessly pursuing him. The steady stream of bullets continued to bounce off the ground and structures around him, some whizzing past his head. Suddenly, Jeremy winced as a round struck his arm and pain screeched in his ears. He desperately leaped through a window into an abandoned, dilapidated building. Aiming his weapon out the window in this direction and then that direction, he hopelessly tried to acquire a target. However, the shadowy assailant wouldn't reveal himself. Roiling with anger, Jeremy fired his weapon haphazardly into the distance until he ran out of ammunition. Then he screamed in defiance toward his covert attacker.

In response to his audacity, a hail of bullets riddled the window frame where he took refuge. After hugging the ground for a moment, Jeremy fled out a backdoor into an open field. Off in the distance, he saw a sandbagged bunker flanked by concertina wire on each side. As he frenziedly struggled to reach the defensive position, he saw American soldiers waving and shouting him on. The closer he got to safety, the faster and harder his heart pounded in desperate anticipation. With a hailstorm of bullets impacting all around him, Jeremy lunged into the opening of the bunker expecting to finally find safety and security. Instead, he found himself immersed in what seemed like thick warm water while gulping down a large mouthful of the foul-tasting liquid. He doggedly flailed about trying to swim to the surface in full combat uniform while his body armor countered his efforts. Struggling to the surface, he found himself treading in an unending pool of blood. As he futilely looked about for a shoreline, the groans and laughter of those he had slain in battle taunted him. He could see some of their faces glaring down at him with vengeful satisfaction.

Persistently treading water with all his strength, Jeremy refused to quit. Finally, exhaustion took its toll. This unrelenting soldier closed his eyes and gasped for one last breath just before the sea of blood engulfed him. As the thick, putrid liquid swallowed him up, he discovered that for some reason he could still breathe. Opening his eyes, he found himself in the Iraqi town of Husayniyah. As he stood within this town located near the Tigris River north of Baghdad, he watched in third person as a military convoy drove past. The convoy conducted route clearance, a procedure designed to locate and destroy IEDs and secure main thoroughfares for safe travel. A Husky vehicle-mounted mine detector led the way followed by most of the sapper platoon and an explosive ordnance disposal (EOD) team. A wrecker concluded the convoy followed by a sapper Stryker vehicle providing rear security for the column.

As the final vehicle past by Jeremy, he saw that SGT Christopher Morningstar and Specialist (SPC) Jeremiah Boehmer manned the two rear security hatchways. Upon graduating from high school, SPC Boehmer enlisted in the Army for adventure. Assigned to the 562nd Engineer Company, Fort Wainwright, Alaska eight months prior to Jeremy, Jeremiah took him under his wing when Jeremy arrived in January 2004 as a private fresh out of basic training. An outgoing young man, Jeremiah had a positive, professional attitude about his military service. His amiable personality surrounded him with countless friends. Having arrived at his first duty station nervous and unsure about things, Jeremy greatly appreciated Jeremiah's camaraderie and guidance. Because Jeremiah always gave his best effort in everything he did, Jeremy highly respected him and would go to the ends of the earth for such as him. After his military service, Jeremiah planned on going to college to become a schoolteacher, wanting to instill knowledge and character into the youth of America.

SGT Morningstar became Jeremy's first military mentor. As a child growing up in Texas, Christopher loved the Army and joined the Junior Reserve Officers' Training Corps (JROTC) in high school. His reverence for and dedication to the Army spilled out onto the soldiers with whom he served. Jeremy often came to him for advice, military knowledge, and direction. Christopher's devotion to the Army compelled him to reenlist a few months after arriving in Iraq when he could have taken an honorable discharge and gone home to his children.

Both of these men profoundly impacted Jeremy's life in their own unique ways. Jeremy held the utmost respect, admiration, and brotherly love for each of them. As their vehicle past Jeremy, he waved and began to call out to them. Abruptly, a loud blast shook the air as an explosion shot flames high into the sky followed by a large plum of black billowing smoke. Using a cell phone, an Iraqi insurgent had detonated an IED near the back end of Morningstar's and Boehmer's vehicle, shredding them brutally with shrapnel and instantly snuffing out their lives. Reaching his hand out to them, Jeremy shrieked in horror, "No!" Regardless of how hard and fast that he tried to run, he couldn't get any closer to the mangled, smoldering vehicle. Suddenly, he felt a burning sensation on his lower legs. Looking down, he saw his uniform on fire from the explosion's burning debris. Seconds later, the flames engulfed him. No matter how much he wanted to reach his comrades, render aid, and save their lives, random hindrances refused to allow it.

While Jeremy lay on the ground consumed by fire and shouting angrily, his surroundings morphed into a forward operating base (FOB). He found himself brooding in deep anger, sitting there glaring at the world around him as rage and loathing gnawed away at his soul. Hatred seethed from his heart. Then he heard a cheery and familiar voice say, "Hey, SGT Smith, what's wrong?" Looking up, Jeremy saw the smiling face of Staff Sergeant (SSG) Bryan Luckey. Bryan never uttered a disparaging word about anyone or anything. He always had a positive attitude in every circumstance.

Grimacing, Jeremy groused, "Why don't we just kill every last person in this forsaken country and get it over with so we can all go home? They're all evil here anyway. Too many good people are dying!"

With a calm and soothing voice, Bryan replied, "Ah, come now. You're looking at this all wrong. Most of the Iraqi people want to live in peace, love and raise their families, and have an enjoyable livelihood just like we do. Most of them don't like or want this war either. Unfortunately, a small remnant of radical extremists is ruining it for everybody. We're here to stop them so that the Iraqis can have a better life and so that the extremists don't come over to our country. Don't allow a few evil people to sour your opinion of the rest of the Iraqi society. Most of them are good people just like you and me." Bryan's words had a therapeutic effect on Jeremy, dissipating the hatred and vitriol that swirled within his heart.

Jeremy looked up again at SSG Luckey. The sun positioned behind Bryan's head bestowed a holy halo upon the saintly soldier. To Jeremy, he seemed a heavenly messenger come to confer encouraging words to his despondent soul. Jeremy greatly appreciated and admired SSG Luckey for his good-natured attitude about everything. Suddenly, the FOB faded to black, and the town of Mosul took its place. Again, Jeremy stood in third person watching a military patrol drive through the treacherous streets of this town located to the north of Baghdad. As he saw SSG Luckey pulling security by standing up out of a rear hatchway of a vehicle, a distant *crack* echoed off the surrounding buildings. Bryan instantly slumped down. An insurgent sniper had shot the saintly soldier in the head. Jeremy could see the light of life slowly dim in the eyes of his wounded friend, who seemed to embody unconditional love for all things and all humanity. Paralyzed by shock, Jeremy couldn't breathe, cry out, or move.

As he blinked, a final roll call memorial formation replaced the streets of Mosul. The unit held the ceremony in honor of their beloved fallen comrade SSG Luckey. The first sergeant (1SG) gave Jeremy the honor of giving the eulogy. At the appointed time, the senior NCO motioned for Jeremy to come forth and speak his words of tribute. However, as Jeremy stood up, his legs hardly moved. Despite his best effort, they felt like lead columns that refused to budge. Looking at the 1SG, Jeremy could see him beckoning feverishly but couldn't hear him. The noise of the solemn gathering eerily became muffled stillness. Suddenly, a high-pitched screech shattered the smothering silence, followed by the loud explosion of a mortar round impacting nearby, preventing Jeremy from honoring his revered comrade.

A quaking jolt brought Jeremy back to his dismal room in Kentucky, as he wrestled with anguish while awash in alcohol. After the darkness worked its will upon him, he suffered from exhausting debilitation and confusion. His inner world in chaos, he lost track of time, the past and present blurred and intertwined. Feeling adrift in dense emotional fog, he couldn't remember who he was before war changed him. Over and over again, he demanded,

"Why them? Why did I make it and not them? They were better than me. I'm a monster." He floundered in the depths of extreme survivor's guilt, hating his preservation profusely. He lunged resolutely over to the desk that held the pistol on which he had worked. Grasping the weapon, he picked it up off the desk. Instantly, his consciousness went blank as he ceased to exist mentally or emotionally. Dense nothingness consumed his soul.

2

A Mother's Heavy Heart

AUGUST 6, 2018, OFFERED plenty of sunshine from the partly cloudy sky that smiled joyfully down upon the cozy little town of Franklin, Kentucky. A temperature of ninety-two degrees gently wrapped the residence in a bearable warm blanket with the day's mild humidity. No rain threatened the beautiful climate. As birds sang emphatically, the people of Franklin went about their normal Monday business. The amiable weather provided some comfort to Jill Smith, who sat next to her husband, Terry, and daughter, Leah. All three gazed solemnly at her oldest child, Jeremy, as he lay there motionless, a stoic expression on his face. Jill took comfort in the thought that over seventy of his military comrades, some from fifteen years ago, came to Jeremy's side in his hour of need. They dropped everything on a moment's notice, spent hundreds, if not thousands, of dollars traveling from as far away as Alaska to be with *Big Country* in his time of distress. The scene reminded her of her hospital stay the day that she gave birth to Jeremy. Her mind drifted thirty-five years into the past as the people and room around her slowly faded into an obscure haze.

♦♦♦

The morning of August 13, 1983, slowly emerged in its stead as she stood in the backyard of her sister's new house. Ice pick in hand, she chipped away at the thick frost that accumulated over time in the fridge-freezer. Pregnant and past her due date, she ignored the frustration with which this grueling work taunted her. Her sister needed help moving into the new home, and defrosting the refrigerator needed to get done. So, she focused on the task at hand and stubbornly ignored the contractions that started around four o'clock that morning.

The arduous work kept Jill's mind off the prospect that she would soon give birth to an infant child who would then be totally dependent on her. Twenty-one years old, this notion scared the fire out of her. Despite the emerging technology of ultrasound, Jill and Terry elected not to know the gender of the baby, though both hoped for a boy. As she toiled away at the ice, she felt as big as the fridge unit in front of her. Fear of motherhood prevented her from fully comprehending the forthcoming and most remarkably unforgettable event that would exceptionally impact her life and deeply change her heart forever. Jill didn't view the prospect of becoming a mom with flowery excitement because her life story had unfolded egregiously. She neither knew the first thing about caring for babies nor what pregnancy would do to her body.

Having little self-esteem or self-confidence because of her childhood experience, Jill often sat on the bed holding Terry's baby picture and beseeched God praying, "Please God, in Your mercy for this baby, please don't let it be like me. Let it be like its daddy." She thought that if she stared at Terry's baby picture long enough and prayed hard enough, then the baby wouldn't be like her. Jill believed in and loved God but had no concept of his love for her. Consequently, she saw no good in herself. Many years later, she came to realize God's love and forgiveness toward her, a testament of his great patience and mercy. But for now, she served God and lived her life as best she knew.

Having read somewhere in the Bible about dedicating the firstborn back to God, she uttered a prayer of dedication throughout the pregnancy. Because she felt a profound sense of duty to foster the child into a good and decent person, Jill desperately wanted to raise the baby well. This gravely concerned her, because one day she would stand before God accountable for how she raised the child with whom the Lord entrusted her. She believed that all people would one day stand before the Almighty to account for how they lived life. So, she wanted to set her child up for success.

Almost three weeks past the due date, Jill suffered from bleeding stretch marks on her stomach because of how huge she had gotten. On the verge of conquering the ice laden refrigerator, her contractions continued to strengthen as the day progressed. Finally, around nine o'clock that night, Jill grabbed her packed bag, and Terry drove her to Community East Hospital in Indianapolis, Indiana. The hospital staff settled Jill into the labor room along with several other women currently in labor, their respective beds separated only by a curtain. Exposed to anyone who happened to walk past, Jill felt uncomfortable by this lack of privacy. As time wore on, the nurses had her walk up and down the hallway where she would have to stop and breath through the contractions.

Jill experienced a difficult labor. To make frustrating matters worse, her regular obstetrician was on vacation, and the fill-in doctor only had two or three deliveries under his belt. He underestimated the baby's weight to be around eight pounds figuring the rest as water and gestational heaviness. Fully dilated, Jill suffered hard labor for eight hours. During contractions, she pushed through as hard as she could. The intense strain propelled her into a tunnel with bright lights whizzing past until blackness engulfed her, thick murky darkness devoid of light, sound, and breath. Despite her feelings of inadequacy, maternal instincts compelled her to travail on the brink of oblivion to bring forth a new life. Terrified that she perched on the verge of death, she found herself once again in the tunnel of lights gasping for air. The doctor wrongly concluded that Jill simply failed to push hard enough. The hospital staff rolled her back and forth repeatedly and instructed her to get on her hands and knees to see if that would help birth the baby. Nothing worked.

The nurses administered an epidural to Jill. Frustrated with the doctor, Terry decreed, "I'm going outside to smoke a cigarette. When I get back, we better be having a baby!" Upon his return, the hospital staff prepped and whisked his wife to the delivery room. The doctor stated that he would try using forceps to assist in the delivery of the baby. If that failed, he would have to perform a cesarean section. Fortunately, the forceps worked. At 12:10 on the afternoon of August 14, 1983, Jeremy Doyle Smith came into the world big, weighing ten pounds, nine ounces. Unknown to Jill at the time, everything about Jeremy's life would be big. Time would reveal a man not only big in stature but also big of heart, mind, and soul. Upon parturition, Jeremy's size caught the doctor by surprise and compelled him to call out for help. The doctor later told Jill that he felt as if someone had hurled a speeding football at him. They laid the newborn child on Jill's stomach. Because of the difficult delivery, she worried that the baby might not make it. During the arduous event, Jill prayed repeatedly, "Please God, let the baby be okay. Please let this little infant be healthy." Then, she heard Jeremy cry for the first time, causing relief to flood her soul as she realized that her newborn child lived. Next, she wanted to count his fingers and toes, joyful that God answered her prayers and gave her the healthy baby boy for which she had hoped.

Jill suddenly realized that her life no longer belonged to her. From then on, it centered around her precious newborn child because God entrusted her with the care and nurturing of this vulnerable little person created in the Lord's image. Fear suddenly gripped her. Feeling woefully inadequate as a mother, she fretted about the unknown odyssey of parenthood on which she now embarked. Uncertainty consumed her as she worried over what mistakes she would make. With the awesome gift of motherhood now placed upon her shoulders, Jill recognized the tremendous mantle of responsibility she forever bore. Despite her misgivings, she determined deeply in her heart that she would raise her son rightly in the eyes of God. At that moment, a new sensation of love flooded her being like never before in her life. Looking deeply into Jeremy's eyes, unshakable maternal affection stirred in Jill's heart as this strange foreign feeling of intense affinity immediately engulfed her.

The nurses cleaned Jeremy up and handed him to Terry, off whose shoulder the newborn lifted his head to look about. He was that strong at birth. Jill, on the other hand, lay utterly exhausted on the delivery bed with a broken tailbone, a bruised lung, and other complications. She lost fifty pounds as a result of accouchement. Despite her condition, Jill marveled at the miracle snuggled in her husband's arms. Another human being had just come from her weak and worn body.

Later in a recovery room, Jill lay in bed fatigued and debilitated as the nurses propped up her arms with pillows and laid Jeremy in them. Holding her first born child for the first time changed Jill's life forever. He made her a mom from this day forward. As he gripped her finger with his entire little hand, she never wanted him to let go, wishing that moment could last forever. Cuddling him against her chest, his warm soft presence soothed her soul. While she counted all his little fingers and toes again, Jill wondered what kind of man he would grow to be. It felt like meeting someone for the first time and experiencing greater love than ever imagined. Jeremy looked at her with the love of an innocent child, the purest love given to humankind on earth. It moved her deeply, and her heart instantly reacted. Tremendous joy and fulfillment revealed a part of her heart that she didn't know existed, an all-consuming, overwhelming love for a vulnerable infant child, her child. A new sensation, she struggled to comprehend this feeling so pure and amazing like nothing else she ever knew. However, this euphoria coupled with great fear because the mantle of motherhood terrified her. Jill didn't want to fail her child. Lost in a fog of confusion, she didn't know how to react and didn't have a clue what to do.

Even though Jill felt like she had just met Jeremy, she recognized his movements right away. When he kicked his leg or stretched out, she could almost feel him again in her womb. She experienced this sentiment even after he grew. Lying on the couch, he stretched his legs or moved a certain way compelling Jill's body to instantly remember. At times, Jill excused herself from the room to shed a tear. She marveled at how attached a mom became to her child. Regardless of race, religion, wealth, education, culture, or upbringing, a mom's heart is forever tied to her child. When Jill first held Jeremy, she instantly connected with him for life.

As Jill ventured into her newly commissioned motherhood, an ominous dread taunted her soul. Because of the difficult labor and delivery of her baby, she received an epidural administration which ceased the pain. As a result, she never felt the delivery of her baby thus obtaining closure of his birth, which seemed all too surreal to her now. This torment of her psyche terrified her as it continually accused her of failure as if Jeremy remained unbirthed with his life in peril. It reminded her of the trauma of that day for a long time to come casting her into profound insecurity. Unable to talk about the labor or delivery for years, she eventually outgrew this anxiety and moved on with her life.

With great joy, Jill and Terry gave Jeremy the middle name *Doyle* in honor of Terry's grandfather on his mom's side. When they told Granddaddy Doyle that Jeremy carried his name and laid that baby in his arms for the first time, the old man wept. Even as an infant, Jeremy profoundly touched lives. A good baby, he ate cereal and slept through the night within a month. He loved to sleep with the blanket over his face. No matter how Jill tucked him in, that blanket inevitably lay gently over his face whenever she peeked in to check on him. A happy baby, he rarely cried or fussed except when teething, which had made him dreadfully sick.

Life didn't afford Jill the luxury of a stay-at-home mom, so she rushed about each workday morning to get Jeremy to the babysitter. She developed a very rigid morning routine in order to get to work on time. Jeremy's day started with Jill standing over his crib with a gleeful smile on her face. She reached down and gently pinched him on the side playfully saying, "Little pincher bug, pincher bug, pincher bug." Sometimes he didn't want to get up and cried in protest. On those days, it pained Jill's heart to force him to awaken, but she had no choice. Finally, nestled in his child safety seat, affixed to the front seat and facing the back of the car, Jeremy gripped his bottle with his left hand and Jill's finger with his right. He trekked daily in this manner to and from the babysitter's, always holding Jill's hand, as well as her heart. Jill treasured this reoccurring ritual, knowing that Jeremy wouldn't always hail as her adorable little man. However, no matter how old he got, when he held her hand, warm tingles shot up her arm straight to her heart. Although she held the large hand of a grown man, her heart always felt the soft, precious hand of an infant.

Often, Jill stood beside Jeremy's crib, cradled him in her arms, and recited the little nursery rhyme, "Bye, baby Bunting, Daddy's gone-a-hunting, gone to get a rabbit skin to wrap the baby Bunting in." She called him her *Baby Bunting*, which he didn't mind until he got older. She also called him

Jeremy Doodle Bug. People lavished a myriad of nicknames upon him: *Boy, Buddy, Buddy Boy, Bubby, Big J,* and *Big Country.*

Jill's mom cherished Jeremy, her first and only grandchild for nearly five years. She cradled the infant boy lovingly in her arms, gently rocked him, and sang *Somewhere Over the Rainbow.* As he got older, Jeremy chimed in, "bo bo bo," when she sang the word *rainbow.* From that time on, she became *Bobo* to all of her grandchildren. She often asked Jeremy, "Who loves you?" The lad emphatically answered, "Bobo!" She then queried gleefully, "Who do you love?" Grinning ear to ear, he again replied, "Bobo!" This started a tradition of endearment between all her grandchildren and her. Later on, if anyone asked Jeremy who he loved, he proudly declared, "Bobo." Bobo had lots of old forty-five records she grew up with, oldies but goodies. Holding music parties, Jeremy and his beloved Bobo listened to music for hours, dancing and singing. They had a tenderly close relationship his entire life. When Bobo passed away in May 2011, Jeremy played his guitar and sang *Somewhere Over the Rainbow* at her funeral.

As a toddler, Jeremy developed a love for toy guns. Jill tried her best to get him to play with the ABC blocks. He would have none of it. He always wanted to play with his toy guns and insisted on taking one to daycare. Jill finally relented. Generous in nature, he let another child play with it much to the toy's demise, for the other child broke it. With his world crashing down around him, Jeremy held the broken toy gun in hand, grimacing in distress with a heart as broken as the toy. To top it off, the daycare center admonished Jill for allowing Jeremy to bring a toy gun with him. Jill explained as best she could to her young child that the daycare didn't allow toy guns even though it allowed other toys. Unable to understand the reasoning for such a policy, his distress grew into consternation. He loved his toy guns.

When Jeremy reached the age of four, Jill and Terry decided to have another child. Although Jeremy was exceptional with structure, a new baby would disrupt their current routine and schedules. To address this, Jill started incorporating a new morning routine into their schedule as if they already had a second child. Every morning, after getting Jeremy ready for the day, Jill took him into the baby's room and taught him his responsibilities as the older brother. She impressed upon him the importance of his role in the baby's life and in the family. She repeatedly confessed that Jeremy would be a good big brother, taking great care of his sibling. Jeremy took it straight to heart. When his sister, Leah Elizabeth, arrived, he emphatically embraced her as his very own. He thought that she hung the moon. Absolutely adoring her, he assumed genuine responsibility for her, fed her, helped change her, watched over her, played with her, and did his best to keep her out of trouble. His love for Leah loomed over her in a big way—big just like he.

A good child overall, Jeremy had his antics. At the age of five, he wanted to have spiked hair. Jill didn't like it but let him do it anyway. He loved to play in the rain and the water sprinkler. One day as he played outside, it began to rain. On this occasion, Jill let him stay out there. He had a grand ole time running around and splashing in the mud puddles. Then he stopped suddenly, turned to look at Jill standing on the porch, and proclaimed loudly, "Honey, hand me the soap!." She burst out laughing. Much to her surprise, he seriously wanted to take a bath out in the rain. With his pleadings tugging at her heart, she sternly denied his petition, though it pained her soul to do so. Finding his spontaneous actions either funny or precious, she treasured them in her heart. One such fond memory occurred when Jeremy came to her and asked if he could get saved. With a melting yet excited heart, Jill knelt with her son at the sofa and prayed with him as he accepted Jesus Christ as his Lord and Savior and committed his life to God.

A skinny child at that time, Jeremy went through a phase where he wouldn't eat. Jill didn't know why he lacked an appetite. He simply possessed no motivation to pick up a fork and eat. Fraught with desperation, Jill literally fed him as she did when he was a young toddler. Fortunately, Jeremy outgrew this quirky anomaly. From the age of seven on, he became a very tall and husky kid full of appetite not only for food but for life, adventure, and competition. Competitive by nature, he insisted on racing Jill to the car when she picked him up from daycare. As a young child, he ran as fast as the wind. Jill let him win most times. However, on occasion, she didn't let him prevail to teach him that life wouldn't always turn out the way he wished. She wanted her beloved son to learn how to face disappointment. This proved a valuable lesson because he railed against losing the race to the car. These losses stung him deeply as he pouted on the way home until he finally learned how to deal with them.

While commuting home, they passed the high school. During late summer and fall, Jeremy saw the high school athletes practicing football. He saw them in pads and uniforms running, passing, and tackling each other. He thought it the neatest thing. Enraptured by the sight, he exclaimed, "Mom, whatever that is, I want to do it!" When he finally got the chance later in his childhood to play football, he learned a valuable lesson in life— things aren't always as glamorous as they seem.

Jeremy started school, a rite of passage that all parents eagerly anticipated. In Jill's case, however, she approached the babysitter's house with trembling lips and tear-filled eyes. Finding it dreadfully hard to leave her children even though the babysitter was a good lady, she backed out of the driveway and headed to work. She pondered how Jeremy's first day would unfold hoping intensely that it would go well for her baby boy. She also felt helpless to affect such an outcome, for the babysitter put him on the bus that morning for the first time, and the babysitter greeted him as he got off the bus that afternoon for the first time. This "joyous event" absolutely broke Jill's heart. With all her being, she wanted to slam on the brakes, throw her car into park right there in the lane of traffic, and run as fast as she could back to the babysitter's house. She deeply yearned to grab her children, take them home, and smother them with love and protection as only a mother could. On the contrary, Terry and she both had to work to make ends meet. Consequently, Jeremy rode the bus to and from school from the babysitter's house rather than from home. The cruel fact that someone else cared for her children made Jill feel dejected. The reality that someone else experienced some of her children's *firsts* taunted her mercilessly. Precious moments that meant little to the babysitter, who soon forgot them, would have meant the world to Jill, priceless memories to cherish for life. Overwhelming guilt and emotional angst devoured her. She cried all the way to work, as well as all that day.

Jeremy did, in fact, have a good first day, attested to by the babysitter. With youthful exuberance that only comes from a child, Jeremy eagerly recounted to his mother how he rode the bus and boldly attended school for the first time without shedding a tear. Emotionally parched, Jill drank in every word and welled up with sincere pride at her son's courage and good behavior without mommy there cheering him. She took comfort in the fact that her baby boy liked school and had a good first day. She took comfort in the fact that they had a good babysitter. Nonetheless, having to work and personally missing out on this experience felt all wrong. Utterly heartbroken, she forevermore would only know of his first day of school from what he and the babysitter told her. Until such things stared her in the face, Jill didn't realize their gravity or impact. With a heart forever connected to her children, she dreaded the circumstances in which life smothered her. Nonetheless, they had bills to pay and well-being to provide for their son and daughter. Despite the angst, Jill continued going to the babysitter's, going to work, and crying her eyes out many times.

A smart student, Jeremy got good grades, above average scores on tests, and stayed out of trouble for the most part. He did, however, go through a phase when he wanted to play at school and at home rather than do his homework. He lied to his parents about completing his assignments. One day, Jeremy's teacher informed Jill and Terry that he had not been turning in his work. Jeremy, however, assured them that he did. Consequently, whenever the teacher's testimony contradicted Jeremy's, he got disciplined by his parents. Although Jill wanted to believe her son, she, along with Terry, tenaciously enforced the rules. After a while, Jeremy realized the futility of his endeavor to have more play time. Not worth the punishment suffered for lying and shirking responsibility, he apologized for his behavior and assured his parents that he would diligently do his homework from then on. He inherently wanted to live life as a good person and determined in his heart to prove that out with his actions, which he did.

Jeremy made many friends at school and looked out for every one of them. One time when a little boy misbehaved, Jeremy begged the teacher to punish him in his stead. Upset because his buddy got in trouble, Jeremy couldn't bear the thought of his comrade undergoing punishment. Empathy personified, his sympathetic heart beat for the welfare of others at an early age. Jeremy came home and told Jill about it. He would truly rather take the suffering upon himself than to see a friend agonize. Later in life, this rare quality would earn him great love and admiration from his brothers-in-arms. It would also, however, heap great agony and grief upon his soul.

Jeremy loved all things army. Terry served in the Army National Guard and had duty one weekend a month and two weeks out of the summer, sometimes more. While a toddler, Jeremy wandered from room to room through the house looking for his dad, who had gone away for military drill. Jeremy loved to play with toy guns, G.I. Joes, and eventually video games. He showed scant interest in building blocks or toy trucks. He liked Hot Wheels and Legos though. Fast cars did enthrall him. But his passion flared for role-playing in the military. He dressed in camouflage every day all the time. He even dressed Leah in camouflage and gave her a toy gun to carry around. He proudly proclaimed, "Look, Mom, we're all soldiered up!." They spent hours building things with Legos for her Barbies, and then Jeremy aggravated them with his G.I. Joes.

When Jeremy turned six years old, he insisted on a camouflaged cake for his birthday party. Subsequently, Jill worked arduously making a dark green cake covered with black, green, and tan camouflage icing. She labored industriously in the kitchen to perfect the colors. Food coloring and Jill had a party of their own. With the cake completed, family and friends gathered for the festive celebration. Consequently, nobody, not even Jeremy, ate the cake because it looked so unappetizing. Although it tasted good, the cake simply looked so awfully disgusting that nobody could bring themselves to eat any.

Jeremy developed a deep crush on Shirley Temple the moment he saw her on television. He loved and swooned over her. If one of her movies aired, he glued his eyes to the TV. He even proclaimed to Jill that he wanted to marry that girl someday. Jill had to monitor his TV watching, though, because if he saw a commercial about children suffering from hunger and poverty, his heart rent in two. The notion of kids starving or living in squalor enraged Jeremy. Crying most inconsolably from anger and disgust, such commercials absolutely tore up his emotions. A good and caring little boy, Jeremy possessed a big and tender heart for humanity. Jill considered the family blessed to have such a lad among them.

The responsibility of fashioning Jeremy into a person of good morals, values, and character continued to weigh heavily upon Jill. She made it her profound personal pursuit to do so, although, at that point in her life, she didn't have a clue how. She turned to the word of God for guidance. Particularly Deut 6:5–7, "And you shall love the LORD your God with all your heart and with all your soul and with all your strength. These words, which I am commanding you today, shall be on your heart. And you shall repeat them diligently to your sons and speak of them when you sit in your house, when you walk on the road, when you lie down, and when you get up."

Disciplining Jeremy when deemed appropriate, Jill used the *spare the rod, spoil the child* method. *Yes* was yes, *no* was no, and *maybe* meant you didn't ask a second time. On the contrary, she did find it easier to spoil her son rather than chastise him. However, to walk such a path meant that she loved herself more than she loved him. Because she took child rearing seriously, she chose the harder road and imposed strict discipline upon her son, correcting and teaching him at every opportunity. God knew better than she about raising children, so she continually pointed Jeremy toward God. She usually directed an irritated Jeremy, pleading for her opinion on a matter, toward Jesus. Jill started this process with prayer when Jeremy was a toddler, prayer at bedtime, prayer at meals, prayer whenever. Growing up, Jill's grandmother, whom everyone called Granny, taught all her grandchildren the Lord's prayer by reciting it with them at bedtime. It stuck with Jill. As a child, she didn't understand the depth and meaning of this encompassing prayer. As an adult, however, she seriously pondered its precepts even to this day. What better way to help her son than to teach him to pray, starting with the Lord's prayer?

Jill read and took to heart Deut 11:18–19, "You shall therefore take these words of mine to heart and to soul; and you shall tie them as a sign on your hand, and they shall be as frontlets on your forehead. You shall also teach them to your sons, speaking of them when you sit in your house, when you walk along the road, when you lie down, and when you get up." She tried lovingly to instill God's word into Jeremy's heart. Not living a perfect life, herself, she felt woefully inadequate but did her best. She struggled with her own insecurities and issues all the while trying to figure out how to raise children. So, she talked about Jesus routinely, often times while standing at the stove fixing supper. Other times, they sat at the kitchen table having Bible studies. If he had a bad day, Jill encouraged him to talk to the Lord.

She sought out scripture that pertained to the situation and tried to make it understandable for her son.

Talking about Jesus became an everyday thing, intricately woven into the moment of whatever was going on. Jill usually replied with, "Well, in the Bible it says," or, "Jesus would want us to." One day, she responded to Jeremy like that. In retort, a frustrated Jeremy declared, "Mom, I don't want to know what Jesus thinks. I want to know what you think!" Doggedly adamant about imparting God's wisdom to her children, she got on their nerves with it at times. Regardless, she resolutely guided them to the Lord—she prayed it with them, talked it with them, and walked it with them as best she could. She got on her knees beside their beds and cried out to God to keep them, lead them, and show them. She fell to her knees beside her own bed and cried the same things for herself. She relentlessly begged God to lay the sins of her children at her feet, a burden she felt that she owned not them, because she was responsible for raising them to live right. She didn't want her children to suffer judgment as a result of her failings as a mom. In such a manner, she lived out every day of her adult life.

One time, Jill struggled, herself, with a situation and just couldn't find peace about it. She grievously pondered why she had to go through it despite living rightly to the best of her ability. In the kitchen, she deliberated with Jeremy about her struggle. He just looked at her and said, "Well, Mom, sometimes storms come to the obedient. Even living right doesn't mean we won't have to endure storms. It rains on the just and the unjust. You know where your shelter is, so get under it, because sometimes, Mom, storms come to the obedient." He said that phrase over and over as if driving it home in her heart, *sometimes storms come to the obedient*. Her little boy fittingly spoke Godly wisdom to her from which she found comfort and vindication for her sagacious tenacity to impart the word of God into her children.

On another occasion, Jill fussed and complained as they ran late one morning about five o'clock, toiling to get out the door, to the babysitter, and ultimately to work. Rushing about, they finally got into the van amidst Jill's unending murmuring and grumbling. Jeremy finally proclaimed, "Mom, you know it's just the devil! Now rebuke him and let's have a good day!" Out of the mouth of babes, God spoke to her through her little boy. *What a blessing and greater than I deserve,* she thought. For his part, Jeremy wanted to live a good life, obey his parents, and make them proud. He didn't want to see them struggle or suffer. He didn't want to see that for anyone.

Jill firmly ensured that Jeremy behaved and showed respect. When bath time came, Jill tolerated no shenanigans and insisted that he get in there and get clean. Terry often teased Jill, razzing her about acting like a drill SGT.

Her actions had merit, however, for Jeremy proved a resolute child. As one of his chores, he emptied every garbage can in the house on trash-pickup day. Jill insisted that he empty every can even if it only possessed a few items of refuse. Not sharing this sentiment with his mom, he argued the futility of throwing away a partially filled bag. They went back and forth over this issue for a season. Choosing her battles wisely, Jill finally relented to his stubbornness, concluding that this particular matter lacked sufficient worth to fight it out to the very end. Recognizing that her compulsive nature motivated her excessive trashcan policy, she admired Jeremy's common-sense approach.

Jill and Terry signed Jeremy up to play football about the age of nine. The coaches made him a defensive lineman, marveling at his tree-stump legs. When he dug his feet in, he stopped everybody. Unfortunately, Jeremy didn't have the desire to hit or tackle the other players for fear of injuring them. The notion of harming someone without proper cause angered him to tears. His genuine heart for humanity compelled him to protest adamantly. He simply didn't want to hurt anyone over a game. The glamour and glory he witnessed as a young child riding past the high school eluded him now. In light of this, the coaches worked diligently to teach him to block, hit, and tackle without mental anger or malice. Eventually, he learned to do these tasks out of duty rather than aggression. Playing without excessive force, he enjoyed and excelled in the sport from that time forward.

In April 1994, the Smith family moved from Indianapolis, Indiana to Franklin, Kentucky, which put them about halfway between both extended families, roughly two hours from each. Jill and Terry rejoiced at the opportunity to move into a new house in a small country town and raise their children away from crowded schools and city crime. Jill and Jeremy cheered as the family vehicle crossed over the Simpson County line. Quite a cultural change, they transitioned to the new community and school as best they could. The venture soon became bittersweet, however. Unfortunately, Jeremy had only a few months to complete the entire year of educational mandates required by Kentucky state law in order to graduate to the sixth grade. Jill argued vehemently against it with the school to no avail. The educators simply wouldn't pass him to the next grade unless he completed their portfolio of mandates. Consequently, Jill worked with Jeremy late into the night on a myriad of occasions during the final weeks of the school year in order for him to satisfy the many requirements. Thankfully, their hard effort resulted in success.

Despite the rough academic start, Jeremy's teachers loved him because he always showed them respect and did his best to be a good student. In time, his eighth grade U.S. history teacher, Mrs. Betty Raines, would become his good friend, a friendship that lasted for life. She, along with other teachers, illuminated for him the tumultuous years of growing up and going through school.

Settling into the new house in the country, Jill insisted that Jeremy and Leah, having only lived in the city until now, go outside and play on a rock pile in the backyard. She wanted them to be kids, play in the dirt, and get filthy. Excited at the prospect, Jill took pictures. Used to only urban surroundings, Jeremy and Leah didn't know what to think of this decree. Much to Jill's chagrin, they milled around the rock pile unsure of how to have country fun. Eventually, they learned to enjoy throwing the Frisbee to each other or playing catch in the yard. At night, they raced off the front porch to the ditch by the road and back with Jill timing them. They learned to find joy in simple things like that. This house became home to them and contained all their childhood memories. They put down roots, something that life didn't afford for Jill when she grew up.

At home, Jeremy loved the old couch that sat in the living room. He called it *the trap* because once he lay down on it, he didn't go anywhere and usually fell asleep. He loved that comfortable old couch and never wanted to get up from it. He missed a lot of rendezvous with his friends because of that cozy old couch. Oftentimes taking naps there, it was his favorite place.

Living only a few hours away now in Kentucky, Granny brought joy and comfort to all who knew her. Seventy years old when Jeremy was born, she cherished her first great-grandchild. Granny lived on a little farm near Terry's mom and stepdad, which made visiting convenient. At the age of four, Jeremy stayed with Terry's mom for a week. She took him over to Granny's for the day. Jeremy had a great time running around and playing outside. As he ran for the porch, he fell and gashed his head on the step, leaving a scar. Granny's farm left its lifelong legacy on his forehead.

When visiting another time, Jeremy and Granny played cards. Granny caught him cheating but kept it to herself for the moment. After the game, Jeremy celebrated his victory, while Granny quietly picked up the cards to put them away. Jeremy emphatically beseeched her for another round, but Granny firmly told him that she didn't play with cheaters. She explained that when people cheat, though it appears that they win for the moment, they really lose in life. Jeremy took that to heart and never cheated again. Granny had a knack for teaching life lessons and left her lifelong legacy on his character.

When Jeremy was about ten years old, another boy at school taunted and bullied him. Initially, Jill's maternal instincts urged her to hunt for this brute and rip out his eyeballs. However, she knew that God wouldn't want that. Submitting to the Lord instead, she taught her son to forgive and pray for his enemies. The bully continued to manhandle and call Jeremy names.

Retaliating only a few times, Jeremy, for the most part, strove to befriend and do good to this person who treated him spitefully. On occasion, Jeremy complained to Jill about the mistreatment. She explained to him that the bully did such mean things because he, himself, had problems and issues with which to deal. Then Jill prayed with her son about the situation.

Around this same time, Jeremy made friends with the little boy next door and a neighbor boy that lived a few streets over. Anyone who took the time to know Jeremy discovered a loyal friend for life, who loved to play video games, shoot off fireworks, and blow up things. Meeting on the school bus, Jeremy also made friends with a boy that lived even further out in the country than he. Jeremy shared with Jill that he worried for this boy who didn't have a good home life. He asked if they could pick him up and take him to church on Sunday. Memories of her own troubled childhood compelled Jill to say yes. When Sunday arrived, Jeremy toiled with the stomach flu. Although deeply miserable, he insisted on going to church along with his friend because he knew it would do the young man good. Without regard for himself, Jeremy wanted the best for his friend that day. Not knowing the entire situation, a woman scolded Terry and Jill for bringing their sick child to church. They took little notice because they knew Jeremy's heart and how important it was to him that a troubled boy got to go to church where Jesus healed the sick and fixed the broken.

The Smith family went to church regularly where the kids participated in the children's ministries. One day, Jill walked through the house and came upon Jeremy laying on the floor playing and making up praise songs to the Lord. He deeply loved God, music, and singing. As a child, he eagerly embraced any opportunity to encourage a family member or friend. Even as a young child, he was the voice of reason to Jill. The Almighty spoke to her out of the mouth of her very own babe, whom God had anointed with divine gifts of empathy and consolation. Jeremy learned to play bass and guitar and did so on the worship team. Jill remembered the very Sunday that he first sang the song *Let It Rain*. From that moment on, every time she heard that song, she saw her fourteen-year-old baby boy standing at the front of the church singing to the Lord with all he had within him. Jeremy, ever hungry for more of God, received the baptism of the Holy Spirit on August 4, 1998, during a revival at church. Jeremy told her that he had a dream of standing next to Jesus Christ who told him that he had something yet to do in life on earth, but that the Lord was coming soon.

Terry and Jeremy frequently went fishing and hunting with Terry's brother and son. Jill called them the *four Smith guys*. Jeremy loved the outdoors, shooting, and hunting. They often had humorous mishaps of falling down a muddy creek bank or slipping into a river. Jeremy's uncle gave him a pair of jungle boots, with which he fell in love. He insisted on wearing them even though four sizes too big. No matter how hard Jill and Terry tried, Jeremy refused to take them off his feet—he loved them that much. Consequently, he stumbled around in oversized boots, his being at a clumsy age not helping. On fishing excursions, the Smith guys routinely heard Jeremy fall with a thump having tripped over a vine in what they now affectionately referred to as his *bozo boots*. Standing on a riverbank, Jeremy's foot would shift inside the boot causing him to lose his footing and plummet down into the water. Smiling as he pulled himself out, he didn't care because he was wearing his beloved jungle boots.

In their younger days, Terry and Jill didn't always make the best financial decisions. They had tough weeks to struggle through because they put themselves in a tight spot financially. At times, they had to roll change to buy groceries for the week. Jeremy took notice of this. After he grew up, he told Jill that he saw them doing it and didn't want anyone to have to go through that. Jeremy grieved for the less fortunate so much that he did things to alleviate their plight. About the age of thirteen, he got his first job harvesting tobacco for the neighbor across the road. He came home each day bone tired and covered in sweat and dirt. Barely able to put one exhausted foot in front of the other, he walked through the door hungry, smelly, and grimy from top to bottom. He earned his first forty dollars ever and spent every penny of it on a less fortunate kid that he knew. Taken aback, Jill declared, "Jeremy, you know how hard you worked for that money. Why didn't you spend some of it on yourself?"

Jeremy looked his mom sincerely in the eyes, smiled, and said, "Mom, chances are good that I will get more money. That family might not." Often, as he stood in the checkout line at the store, he paid for the items of the people in front of him when it became apparent that they didn't have enough money themselves. He came home from Walmart one day a bit irritated by the ill-fortune that others experienced. When Jill asked what bothered him, he replied that while in line at the store, a young couple with a baby checked out in front of him. They began to put stuff back because they didn't have enough money to buy both the groceries and the baby items that they needed. With a heart rent in two, Jeremy spent his money ensuring that they got everything that they needed. Consequently, he didn't buy any of the things that he went to the store to get for himself. He always did acts like this for those less fortunate. One time, he even gave his really nice, expensive watch to someone who liked it but could probably never afford such a timepiece. He was almost generous to a fault.

During Jeremy's freshman year in high school, unbeknownst to Jill and Terry at the time, some older boys on the football team bullied their gentle giant of a son. As Jeremy concentrated on playing football to the best of his ability, these upperclassmen harassed and humiliated him. With hardly a thought for himself, Jeremy refused to tell his parents for fear that it would cause them dismay. He felt that they had enough burdens in life at the time, so he chose to quietly endure the ordeal for his parents' sake. As fate would have it, Jeremy in time made friends with an upperclassman who also played football. His newfound friend stood up for him and put an abrupt stop to the whole nefarious situation. They remained friends for life.

When teenagers, if Jeremy or Leah got upset about something, Jill sat them down and wouldn't let them leave until they discussed the matter. Jill usually didn't change her mind about the situation or let them have their way, but she always wanted to hear what they had to say. On one such occasion when Jeremy was upset about something, Jill handed him a couch cushion and told him to take his anger out on the pillow. She declared this a safe and constructive way to vent his anger. Jeremy flipped the cushion into the air and punched it tumultuously, catapulting it across the room. True to its unintended mark, the now rogue cushion knocked over and broke a living room lamp. The agitation of breaking the lamp propelled Jeremy into a deeper sulky glower. That ended Jill's homemade-therapy exercises. She finally learned that if she quietly sat in the living room, her kids would come in and start telling her about their day or about something that bothered them. She wanted them to feel comfortable telling her anything.

While growing up, Jeremy didn't like his middle name *Doyle.* Then he learned that Jill and Terry named him after his great-grandfather and how the old man wept for joy when first cradling the infant Jeremy in his arms. From then on, he carried that name proudly. He also took great pride in his last name of *Smith.* His parents imparted to him the value of a good name and that their family had good standing within the community. They encouraged him not to tarnish the reputation of the family name but to live a life that would herald it. The Smith men lived honorable lives, many answering the patriotic call to fight for freedom and the republic when beckoned. His great-grandfather served in WWI, his grandfather in WWII, his uncle during the Korean conflict, and his dad in the National Guard for many years. Jeremy took this to heart. When things got tough, Jeremy dug in with grit and determination, as if carrying the Smith name empowered him to overcome anything. If someone commented on his tenacity, he often replied, "Last name Smith, ain't it?"

Nevertheless, as with all people, Jeremy got discouraged at times in his life. When he got his driving permit, Jill took him out one day to practice. While going through the Walmart parking lot, he ran a stop sign. Jill scolded him for not paying attention and decried all the tragic things that could have happened. Jeremy responded with a blank look on his face and a brooding attitude in his soul. After returning home, Jill found him sitting on the floor in his bedroom with the driving permit in front of him. She asked, "Jeremy, what's wrong?"

Holding himself to a standard of excellence that he failed to meet, he looked up at her with resolute eyes and replied staunchly, "Mom, I feel like a loser who failed to do his best. I'm tempted to tear up my permit." Jill experienced one of the few times that Jeremy revealed his raw feelings. Often, he kept his personal disappointments to himself because he didn't want to burden others with his discontents. That exceptional day, however, he shared his feelings with Jill. Sitting there together on the floor, they talked for a long time.

Jill shared her love for music with Jeremy. They would listen to each other's musical preferences even in those cases where they didn't particularly like what the other enjoyed. Jeremy once told Jill, "Mom, I love that you accept me for who I am, even the music that I like." In many instances, though, they did shared a common fondness for the same music. She gave him a Simon and Garfunkel cassette tape. Classic hits like *The Sound of Silence, Bridge Over Troubled Water*, and *Mrs. Robinson* played over and over in his room, especially when he went to bed.

One day, Jeremy declared that he wanted to learn how to play the bass guitar. Listening to the radio in the car, he would exclaim, "Mom, do you hear the bass? Listen. Do you hear the bass? That's what I want to play!" Jill and Terry gave him a bass guitar and an amplifier for his sixteenth birthday. Someone gave him a self-teaching video cassette with which he taught himself how to play the instrument. He watched it repeatedly and practiced until his fingers bled. Blessed with a natural talent, he felt the melody as if part of him and played from his heart. He also learned to play acoustic and electric guitars, as well as read music. Writing his own tunes, he played the bass guitar in a band of high school classmates and with the worship team at church. Often Jill played the piano and accompanied Jeremy on the guitar. They did this for hours upon hours over the years.

Jeremy also possessed a phenomenal talent for singing. As he got older, he moved people emotionally with his voice when he sang. Sometimes, as Jill got ready for work in the morning, Jeremy sang the Frank Sinatra song *That's Life*. He sounded so good that she often yelled out for him to sing it again. Music became his outlet where he found peace. Eventually, it would become his therapy.

At the age of sixteen, Jeremy earned educational credit for working an after-school job at Sonic. Returning home one day after work, he changed out of his greasy clothes and proclaimed that he would do his own laundry.

He stated that he was old enough to take care of it himself and that Jill had enough work to do around the house in addition to her full-time job. He didn't want to impose unnecessary burdens on her. Although Jill needed his clothes to make full loads when she did laundry, she acquiesced, proud of her son's newfound maturity in taking personal responsibility. He did his own laundry most of the time thereafter.

Late summer 2001 changed Jeremy's life forever. On August 3, dear Granny passed away eleven days before his eighteenth birthday. He loved her deeply and shared with Jill that her passing nearly killed him inside. All their hearts broke when that precious old lady died. Jeremy loved God and family profoundly. Although he stumbled, strayed, and got lost at times, he always knew where to find the home of his soul—in Jesus. He often said that nothing counted more to him than blood family. He loved his sister immeasurably, as well as his parents. The four of them intertwined and became as unbreakable as a tightly wound rope. He summed up his view of life with these adages: be a few minutes late in order to enjoy life and your talents; go play in the rain and get your good clothes dirty; you can always make more money, but you will never have any more time for family and friends.

Before he recovered from the loss of his precious Granny, September 11 came—the day the world changed, defining cowardice on the part of terrorists and valor on the part of first responders and average Americans. Pursuant to the attack, they all knew that in short order the country would declare war in retaliation to this barbarism. Jeremy came into this world blessed to live in the greatest country. As he aged, he marveled at the freedoms, liberties, and opportunities the United States afforded its citizens. This made him a patriot through and through. He often extolled the many blessings that availed to Americans and was grateful and proud to be one. He honored the flag and shed a tear when he heard the National Anthem. He knew of the sacrifices that his forebears made for this great country and availed himself to join their ranks. The United States meant that much to him. Consequently, he took 9/11 very personally.

A year later, Jeremy came through the back door as Jill sat at the kitchen table. He opened the fridge, reached in to get a drink, and spoke from the other side of the refrigerator door, "Mom, I joined the Army today." A moment of cold still silence followed. In quiet desperation, Jill conceded to herself that she knew this day would come. She tried to prepare herself for the inevitability that one day her children would grow up and make their own decisions. However, such an aspiration perpetually dwelt just beyond a mom's reach. Jill's heart slid into her shoes. Regardless, she loved her son indescribably and believed in him. So, despite her maternal impulse to always protect her precious baby boy, she trusted his judgment and stood behind his decision.

As Jeremy peeked from around the refrigerator door, Jill forced a smile and expressed her full support. She reminded him of 9/11, pointed out that he would probably end up in combat, and asked him if he was sure about it. She pondered if a nineteen-year-old could really be sure of such a thing and then questioned how a forty-year-old mom could be sure. She remembered the five-year-old boy outraged on behalf of hungry children and the nine-year-old boy who didn't want to hurt anyone in football. How could his heart for humanity reconcile killing another person in combat? This reality loomed unavoidably because people inevitably died in war. Jeremy solemnly walked over to Jill and sheepishly said, "I didn't really join the Army today. I just wanted to see how you would take it."

Jill sighed with relief as if the Rock of Gibraltar lifted off her shoulders. Jeremy wanted to see how his mom would handle such a monumental event in their lives. Many might believe his unconventional method disrespectful, but Jill appreciated her son's consideration expressed in his own unique way. Having passed the test, she knew that this day awaited her in the near future. As a result of repeated Iraqi violations of the Gulf War cease-fire agreement and consistent Iraqi support for and financing of international terrorism, the Iraq War commenced March 20, 2003. America, land of the free and home of the brave, found itself in a second war to combat terrorism. Cable news offering continuous war coverage, the Smith family anxiously watched practically nothing but, especially the coverage of Jessica Lynch, the first rescued prisoner of war since World War II. Recovering in a hospital in Germany, she was nineteen years old, the same age as Jeremy, who then, himself, enlisted in the Army on April 7, wanting to do his part in defending freedom and his country from tyranny.

Historically, the month of August presented life-changing events to the Smith family on ordinary sunny days—the year 2003 no exception. Jeremy turned 20 years old on August 14. On August 20, he shipped out for basic training at Fort Leonard Wood, Missouri. Earlier that day, Jill watched from the porch, while he ran laps around the property, as he did day in and day out losing weight and getting into shape for military service. Later that day, he stretched out on his belly on the living room floor and played video games, like he did a gazillion times in the past. Jill sat on the couch and drank in every moment of his image, as he pressed the buttons of his game console. She lovingly said, "I'm sure going to miss you, Jeremy." He replied, "I'm really going to miss you too, Mom."

Jill pondered that after Jeremy's fifteen-week training, her baby boy would cross over into manhood. He would grow up while away serving in the Army, rather than at home where she could watch over and protect him. She knew that the person who would come home on leave wouldn't be her child-son but a man, grown and changed. After this day, she would never see her baby boy again. A bitter-sweet moment, deeply massive pride and joy comforted her heart while the prospect of sorely missing him tormented it. Jill contemplated his compassionate soul for humanity and his unfathomable love for family, friends, and country. He knew no other way but to profoundly care for other people. What did the future hold for him? Would he emotionally handle the requirement of soldiers to fight and kill in combat? Would he endure the psychological trauma inflicted by the evils of war?

Jill tried to take her mind off these quandaries by playing music with her son. She graced the ivory and ebony keys, while Jeremy made his guitar sing, as they did a myriad of bygone days. When they finished, Jeremy placed the guitar picks on the TV as always, and there they remained for years to come during his military service. No one had the heart to move them. Jill carefully dusted around the guitar picks using great care not to disturb them. The sight of them gave loving comfort to her heart. She could almost hear her baby boy playing the guitar.

As Army recruiter, Sergeant First Class (SFC) Palecki, slowly pulled into the driveway in a government car, Jill burst into sobbing not ready to let go of her baby boy. When the SFC entered the house, Jeremy introduced him. He took one look at Jill and queried with concern, "Ma'am, are you okay?"

Jill shot back through her tears, "No, I'm not okay. My boy is leaving today!" Jill couldn't stop crying.

Having seen this scenario time and again, he nodded with compassion in his eyes and understanding in his heart. SFC Palecki handed Jill his card and said, "If you need anything, let me know. I hope you will be all right."

Jill retorted, "No, I won't be all right. You are taking my baby boy. I will never be all right!"

The SFC proceeded to take measurements of Jeremy to ensure that he met body-weight standards. Part of Jill hoped that he didn't. Hugging his mom heartily, Jeremy said, "I love you, Mom." She returned the affection. He then picked up his bags and walked out the door eager to start his new adventure. As the next chapter of his life lay before him, he anxiously yearned to get to it. Wanting to be a soldier all his life, Jeremy's dream unfolded right before Jill's tear-filled eyes. He didn't understand that once he walked out that door, the innocent young Jeremy would never come back. In his stead would return a seasoned man knowledgeable of the ways of this wicked and troublesome world. With a tormented soul, Jill understood it completely as her heart broke in ways that she never knew possible.

Jeremy didn't comprehend the depth of his mom's grief. In his mind, he only embarked on the fifteen-week journey of basic training. Then he would return home on leave, the three years of his enlistment a distant prospect at that juncture. He felt as if he held the world in his hand. While the two men made their way down the walkway to the car, Jill glued her eyes on Jeremy. As the recruiter got in the car, Jeremy opened the passenger car door, stopped, and looked back at Jill, a scene engraved in her memory forever. He raised that big hand of his up in the air, gave her a vigorous wave, and said with a huge smile on his face, "See ya later, Mom!" By stepping into the car, the innocent young Jeremy stepped away from Jill for all time. When the car door closed, the click of the latch assembly hung in the air for what seemed like an eternity. Jill realized from the porch that she would never again see her Baby Bunting Boy, her Jeremy Doodle Bug, for that chapter of his life closed along with the car door. Just like that, her sweet-hearted boy vanished. As the car drove off, destiny began to scribe the opening pages of the next chapter of Jeremy's life—that of a soldier answering the call of duty and serving his beloved country, the life of which he dreamed.

3

Offerings Upon the Altar

Fifteen weeks later, Jill and Terry wandered the parade grounds of Fort Leonard Wood, Missouri, after Jeremy's graduation from a combined basic/advanced individual training course. Jill desperately looked for her son in an unending sea of camouflaged uniforms. Consequently, a young soldier accidentally bumped into her. Impatient and frustrated, she gave the young man a dirty look and continued searching for her baby boy. After taking a few steps, she heard a voice behind her declare, "Mom, it's me, Jeremy! Why did you keep walking?" Jeremy had lost so much weight that Jill looked him square in the eyes and didn't recognize him. Once she realized that she stood face to face with her son, she lunged forward and gave him the heartiest hug. Jill and Terry brought their boy home during Christmas prior to his departure for his first duty station at Fort Wainwright, Alaska.

While visiting at home on leave, Jeremy thanked his parents for the strict, stern upbringing, which helped him as an adult in the world, especially at basic training. Jill and Terry strove to raise their children right, teaching them about God, about good values, and to live a decent life. Both Jill and Terry came from broken homes, so they made sure that their children didn't. Determined to ensure that Jeremy and Leah experienced a better childhood than either of them, they did their best to provide a stable home no matter what life threw at them. Regardless of how hard things got, they taught their children to never quit.

Jeremy became a combat engineer referred to as a *sapper*. He would eventually become highly efficient with demolitions. While in Iraq, when more senior soldiers failed to bring down a building, Jeremy went in, repositioned the explosives, and successfully demolished the structure. He just loved that sort of stuff. Many of his comrades called him *Big Country*, another nickname in a vast litany of sobriquets. His favorite drill instructor, Drill SGT Macintosh, gave him that nickname during physical training (PT) in the fifth week of basic.

Jeremy deployed to Iraq from August 2005 to December 2006. Every day, Jill prayed for the safety of her son, while angst weighed heavily upon her heart as if to cast it deeply into a dark unending abyss. When he came home on leave in December 2005, Jill could barely contain her excitement— her Buddy Boy home alive and in one piece! Terry, Jill, and Leah always picked him up or saw him off at the airport without fail. When they met him in the terminal, Jill ran toward him as fast as she could the moment that she laid eyes on him. She couldn't wait to hug her baby boy, to feel him alive in her embrace. Wrapping her arms emphatically around him, the two of them nearly fell. Jeremy heartily hugged her back, anxious and excited to see them. There he stood all *soldiered up*, as he used to say, walking proudly and tall.

Granny collected poems and, when Jeremy was a baby, gave Jill one such writing titled *Your Name,* written by Edgar A. Guest. She asked Jill to give it to Jeremy when he became an adult. Its verses spoke about the value of a good name, good reputation, and a good life. Jill put it in a picture frame, along with a picture of Jeremy and Terry, and treasured it throughout the years. During her childhood, Jill always wanted to have a good family name. Unfortunately, her dad didn't establish a good name for himself. An absentee father and an alcoholic, he treated people abusively. Consequently, she didn't want to own his name. When Jill married into this Smith family, she felt honored to now belong to a family with a good name. She gave the poem to Jeremy that December when he came home on leave from Iraq. He cherished it for the rest of his life. The poem emphasized the worth of maintaining good character so as to establish a good name among the community and of passing that good name on to the next generation.

Jeremy returned to the Iraq War January 2006 for another year. Upon his ensuing homecoming that December, everything changed. War didn't end when the warrior came home. Another conflict began on the home front against a more elusive nemesis. Jill soon learned that precept as one day Jeremy looked at her with deep sincere eyes and uttered, "The war is not over, Mom. Trust—I don't remember what that is."

On the way home from the airport, Jeremy sat in the front passenger seat alert and constantly scanning the road and ditches. He shared with his family that over there even a simple looking pothole could mean death by IED. His exposure to combat trained him to watch out for such devices of demise. Deeply ingrained in his psyche, doing such had become second nature to him. Jill noticed almost immediately that her son lost his sense of well-being and safety that we Americans take for granted. Jeremy never fully recovered that sense of security ever again, a sacrifice laid upon the altar of freedom. Dismayed by the mental angst of her baby boy, Jill affixed her eyes on him from the back seat. As mom, she had all the remedies to heal a distraught heart. With encouraging words and a loving embrace, she always had the ability to soothe her children's troubled souls. For the first time in her life, Jill sat dumbfounded and inept at what to do, completely at a loss, totally helpless. With a heavy heart, she reached out and touched his shoulder. Jeremy immediately grabbed her hand and held it firmly the entire ride home.

When they pulled into the driveway, Jeremy drank in the sight of *home* with his parched eyes that had wandered through the dry wilderness for sixteen months. When the vehicle came to a stop, he never spoke a word but got out of the car and walked across the driveway to the front yard. He fell to his knees in grateful disbelief, laid his body flat to the ground, and kissed the turf. Jill's heart melted as tears welled in her eyes. From that moment on, that piece of yard became hallowed ground to her. Standing up, Jeremy confessed, "I promised myself that if I made it home alive, then first and foremost, I would kiss the sacred ground of home—America."

Even at home, Jeremy found it impossible to relax. He sat on the edge of his seat, every seat. He didn't scoot or lean back into whatever he sat on, not even the trap. This caused concern for Jill. Something didn't seem right. Little did she know that things would never be the same again. No matter what he did, Jeremy remained continually vigilant, constantly at the ready to confront unseen threats. He even watched TV on the edge of his seat, refusing to throw his arm up across the back of the couch and get comfortable. He sat with a straight back and kept his feet and knees together. Not a single muscle in his body seemed to relax. Jill had never seen him like this before. It took a long while before Jeremy finally leaned back when he sat down. Relief flooded Jill's heart the first time that she saw this. Finally, things were getting back to normal, or so Jill hoped. Tragically, though, fate had other intentions.

Jeremy continued to be hypervigilant and easily startled. On one occasion, Jill kissed his cheek, making a loud smooching smack. Jumping at the sound, he tensed up and took several minutes to calm down. Unanticipated noises or walking into a presumably empty room and suddenly seeing someone there startled him. Jill learned to minimize her physical show of affection and gave her son space, another offering upon the altar. One day, when Jeremy picked Jill up from work and took her to lunch, he constantly jerked the steering wheel as he drove. Embarrassed, he kept apologizing for the uncontrollable nervous tick. Jill noticed that external sights caused his subconscious and his body to react beyond his control. She could tell that it troubled him greatly.

He nervously scanned parking lots and sat with his back against the wall in restaurants, evaluating everything and everyone as threats. By the grace of God, most Americans never spent a prolonged period of time in a continually hostile environment. As a result, the average American couldn't relate to the plight of those who did. Because of the sacrifice and suffering of combat veterans, typical Americans lived in relative safety, shielded and protected by freedom and liberty. Americans enjoyed this protective hedge taken for granted but wrought and maintained by those who served in combat.

Throughout the years, Jill and Jeremy relished shopping together. They decided to go to the shopping mall one day. During the entire trip, he kept tugging her arm and pulling her back away from people or would get in front of her to shield her from perceived potential danger. They tried to have lunch in the food court, but the amount of people that Jeremy attempted to assess as friend or foe overwhelmed him. They cut the excursion short and simply went home, both saddened by the outcome. With a despondent soul, Jill looked at her son sitting there sullen and quiet. Shopping had been one of their most favorite things to do together but now became intensely stressful for him. Far too taxing on his nerves, that enjoyable activity ceased to exist for them. Unfortunately, Jeremy never enjoyed shopping in crowded places again, another sacrifice laid upon the altar of freedom.

General comments and minor inconveniences often easily angered Jeremy. The first few times when Jeremy talked about what happened over there and shared his feelings about it, Jill relished the opportunity to offer comfort and healing to her baby boy. She replied that she understood his plight. Gravely aggravated, Jeremy immediately retorted, "How could you understand? You were never there! You didn't live through it!" Jill's heart sank. All she wanted was to console her son. Instead, she unwittingly inflamed his inner turmoil. Completely at a loss for how to help, she walked on eggshells around him, carefully choosing her words and responses. As she pondered his rebuke, she realized that she didn't, in fact, understand. Nobody could truly understand unless they went through combat. Jill recognized that the sweet, tender, gentle side of Jeremy seemed buried under a mountain of anger. He displayed such negative emotions first and foremost. He told Jill that his anger, as his main survival tool, helped him endure over there. Although home in a safe and secure place, he felt the constant compulsion to fight and survive.

On another occasion, Jeremy flew into a rage when coming home to see that the family displayed a tattered American flag outside their home. He ranted that his fallen brethren returned home within a casket draped with a pristine American flag. How could his own family show such disrespect to the country for which he suffered so greatly. Unbeknownst to Jeremy, that particular flag began flying in front of the house on the day that he left for war. Terry, Jill, and Leah cried under that flag. They prayed their beloved soldier home under that flag. It became their *banner* over him, a shield of protection wrought from prayer and faith.

Nonetheless, they replaced tattered Old Glory with a fresh immaculate one, since Jeremy couldn't see what the weathered flag meant to his family. Fighting back tears, Jill immediately went to the store and bought the new flag which they put up that day in honor of their son and his comrades-in-arms. An unblemished flag flew in front of the house ever since. Upon seeing the new flag, Jeremy never uttered a word. He simply nodded in contented approval as if they corrected a terrible wrong, thus allowing his soul to let out a huge sigh of relief. Jeremy would passionately fight and die to protect the freedom, rights, and liberties of any American, even though it angered him that they took these blessings for granted, ignorant of the high price that he and his brothers paid on their behalf. He would never again enjoy a sense of well-being and security himself, so that other Americans could.

This event wounded Jill because she lamented that her son would think that they would ever do anything to hurt him. Tattered Old Glory now rested in the closet, with great sentiment for it dwelling in Jill's heart. The flag quietly and proudly resided there since the day of Jeremy's outburst. Sometimes Jill spent time reminiscing over tattered Old Glory, admiring and caressing it as past feelings and memories flooded her being, but she never moved it from its final resting place. As much as Terry, Jill, and Leah couldn't understand what Jeremy went through in war, so too he didn't understand what they went through at home travailing over him in love, prayer, and grief until the day that they saw his precious face return from war.

Since he did, in fact, come back from war, Jeremy wrestled with survivor's guilt because he couldn't understand why soldiers whom he considered better than he had died while he lived. This self-imposed condemnation weighed heavily upon his soul. Two soldiers whom he greatly admired died on Superbowl weekend in 2006. As a result, Jeremy couldn't bring himself to watch football for years. The Smiths had always been a football family. Jeremy played football as a child. They loved to watch professional football games together. Watching the Superbowl in a big family get-together became a tradition that yielded lots of food, cheering, and fun. After 2006, Jeremy had great animus toward football. If his fallen brothers couldn't watch it anymore, than neither would he. Over time, Jeremy rationalized that his fallen comrades wanted him to enjoy the blessings that they paid the ultimate price to secure. In honor of them, he began to watch football with his family and friends again. Such camaraderie did him good.

Jeremy couldn't sleep much at night either because of nightmares, horrific ones, which worsened over the years. He moaned dreadfully and cried out gruesome groans, almost indescribable, that protruded from horrendously deep and painful grief. Gut-wrenching to hear, they made Jill cry herself. Jeremy often dreamed of burning alive, getting shot, or the blood of the slain smothering him. He awakened in a panic, patting himself down as if on fire, totally soaked in sweat, and shaking frantically. At times, Jill tapped on his door or opened it slightly to say, "Jeremy, Jeremy honey. It's Mama." Sometimes, that made the crying stop. Other times, he woke up and looked at her, wide-eyed in total confusion for a few seconds.

Some nights, Jeremy got up and watched Care Bears, his favorite show as a child, desperately hoping that it would transport him to a calmer time of life that existed long ago before the anguish of combat came to be, a safe world where others looked out for you and cared for one another. On occasion, he fell back to sleep void of dreams. If he slept four hours without a nightmare, Jeremy considered it a good night's rest. Greatly embarrassed by all this, he asked Jill if she had heard him crying at night. He desperately didn't want his mom exposed to the grief of it all.

Jeremy hardly spoke of his combat experience in detail. He found it difficult to relive the horrors that he endured. Soulfully wounded, he withdrew from any emotional connections with others, even his family. This constituted the greatest angst for Jill. Jeremy used to talk about almost anything with her, not so after his combat tours. He seemed irate and distant most of the time. The loss of their close relationship became another offering upon the altar. He didn't want to expose his mom to the atrocities of war or tell her in detail of the times when he had to kill another human being. Because of such feelings, he seldom shared with anyone what he went through over there, especially Jill. His love to protect and shield her from what he had endured in war and the pain he silently suffered far outweighed his desire to ease his own burden. She agonized over this for years. Maybe Jeremy didn't want to shock and disappoint her with some of the malevolent things he had to do in combat. She concluded that deep down he withdrew to protect her. She tried desperately to get him to understand that she would gladly bear any sorrow if it would help him. She would take on any burden to lighten his load.

One day, Jill found Jeremy standing by the piano holding and staring at his rifle scope that he looked through while at war. He didn't like the ones that the military issued, so he bought and used a better one. As she walked up, he held it out and said, "I'm giving this to you today, Mom."

At a loss for words, she took it and placed it with her other most treasured things that she kept on top of the piano. Jill perceived this as Jeremy's way of sharing his war experience with her without using words. She now possessed the scope through which he witnessed atrocities untold. She often held it in her hands and prayed for God to heal the hellacious memories burned into Jeremy's psyche. At times, she looked through it, hoping for a glimpse into her son's soul. Sometimes Jill found him there holding it again in his hand, ruminating events that he declined to share with his mom. Regardless of how much he may have wanted such, he refused to do so for her own protection. He forbade the things that seared his soul to scorch hers. However, she would gladly allow anything to char her heart if it would ease his pain in any way.

Nevertheless, Jeremy became overly critical toward Jill. If she fussed about the heat of the day, he sharply admonished, "At least you aren't fighting in over one-hundred-degree heat in seventy pounds of gear!" If she appeared to take things for granted, he became terribly upset because his brothers paid a high price for her freedom, liberty, and blessed life. What right did she have to complain about anything? Did she not properly appreciate or fully acknowledge the ultimate sacrifices paid for her comfortable, albeit not perfect, life? Jeremy saw firsthand how expensive this price was. He, himself, continued to pay that price with his own tormented life. Years later, Jeremy finally realized that life was tough on everybody one way or another. Everyone felt pain, grieved, and agonized at times while navigating their way through this world. He eventually apologized to Jill for his unfair judgment and harsh treatment of her. His inherent compassion and selfless focus on others began to whittle its way out from beneath the volcano of anger raging within him.

After getting out of the Army, Jeremy didn't act or look the same. He lost his innate empathy for others and his sharp military comportment, looking sloppy most of the time. He kept people at a distance by projecting himself as a big, gruff, ugly guy. He had this angry, wounded look on his face and distant gaze in his eye that revealed a debilitated soul injured by a myriad of terrible trials and tribulations. Despite all this, Jill still saw in him the good, caring person she knew her son to be. She tried to comfort Jeremy by pointing out that the Army trained him to kill the enemy in war. Unfortunately, the enemy consisted of other people. Going to war to protect one's country meant killing other human beings, an unavoidable fact. Jeremy had some idea of the horrors of war beforehand. Tragically, he didn't realize how deeply the traumas of combat would embed into his psyche now that he had an intimate firsthand knowledge of it all.

Jill continued to share Bible scripture with Jeremy and encourage him as she felt led to by the Holy Spirit. One day when Jeremy wrestled with the dark place, Jill sent him a text that read, "There is no fear in love. Perfect love will cast out fear. If you are feeling burdened and afraid, you can trust God's love."

Jeremy replied, "Mom with the win! I've been anxious all day! I needed that. You're the best!"

Another time when the darkness overcame Jeremy, Jill told him, "Consider the birds of the air. If God takes care of them, he will surely take care of you." Her encouragement gave him peace. Jill persistently yet gently talked about the Lord with Jeremy even at times when he didn't want to hear it.

Often times, he struggled to get his life back on track. One evening, he sat in the breezeway between the house and the garage and pondered his situation. As Jill went out to talk to him, she prayed for God's guidance. She felt that the Lord told her he would soon give Jeremy beauty in exchange for his ashes. She lovingly said to her baby boy, "Son, the Lord is going to give you beauty for the ashes of your life. All you must do is let everything go and give it all to him. He is standing right beside you with his arms outstretched to take it all from you."

Jeremy stood up with tears in his eyes and said, "Mom, I've been reaching out. I can't hear a word. He's going to have to do something for me soon." Then he walked away dejected.

Sometime later, Jill heard a person speaking on TV about beauty for ashes. The person said that the ashes represented all the loss in one's life. She knew that God didn't fail her that night she spoke to Jeremy about it. She knew that God would follow through on his word.

As the years of his military service and combat experience progressed, Jeremy's music preferences got darker and darker. Eventually, he got into Metallica and other bands whose music bothered Jill. As in her son's younger days, she listened to his choice of music with him even though this time it disturbed her to do so. Since Jeremy couldn't communicate with Jill directly in a heart-to-heart conversation, he did so through the music. He used songs to tell her deep laden things dwelling within him that he couldn't say to her in person. They talked and texted each other through songs. Jill texted Bible verses to him for encouragement. One time, she sent him a song that said *be still and know that I am God*. Sadly, however, he replied with a song about driving on a back-country road, drinking whiskey, sniffing cocaine, and soon ending up in a casket. Although an ominous way of sharing his mental and emotional state, Jill embraced it since it offered a way for her to somehow connect with her son.

One evening, Jeremy went to his truck to listen to music, something he enjoyed doing. Once out there, he texted Jill inviting her to come join him, skeptical that she would. Upon her opening the truck door, he welcomed her with a pleasantly surprised look on his face. Genuinely glad that she accepted his request, he sat there happily listening to music with Jill. Although they didn't talk much, he greatly appreciated her spending time with him despite his musical preference.

Jill struggled to remember Jeremy as a five-year-old child because they had traveled a grueling road through life, filled with a myriad of painful ordeals. His childhood seemed a lifetime away, now that she saw her son so terribly broken from fighting terrorism and defending freedom and liberty. Beforehand, she didn't realize the high cost of such blessings. It gave her a greater appreciation for life in the United States as she pondered all the lives lost and broken to preserve freedom and liberty over the past two hundred forty plus years. She grieved over her son's shattered disposition and tried to take comfort in the fact that he became thus by fighting for a righteous and noble cause.

Jill, along with Terry and Leah, knew in their hearts that Jeremy would return home from war a different person. Although they each had their own idea of how, none of them accurately fathomed the cavernous depth of that transformation. They each conceptualized how they thought he would change. Yet, their expectations and concerns fell far short of harsh reality. Since none of them experienced combat themselves, they had no way of remotely knowing how war impacted a person or how to relate to such a one. Just like only those women who had given birth to a child truly knew the experience, no one could know the impact that war had on a person except the combat veteran. Having little or no knowledge of the matter, they could, at best, only form a superficial idea. As a result, they made so many mistakes.

Jill's first was not knowing about what the soldiers truly dealt with in war, the atrocities they saw, and the horrific events in which they participated. If she had studied it, then she would at least have had a better understanding of what to expect. In child birthing, she knew beforehand the process, how to breathe, and of the contractions. Concerning what her son might have experienced in war, however, she was clueless. The depths of his suffering ran so deep that Jeremy didn't understand it himself. He called himself a *monster* for killing so well in battle. Jill's baby boy was anything but a monster. The Army had trained him to kill for a just and righteous cause. There was a time for war and a time for peace, a time to kill and a time to heal. There came times in this world when good people had to stand up to and fight evil. She truly felt in her heart that what Jeremy did in war didn't make him a lesser man. She had raised him well. His last name was *Smith*. Unfortunately, Jeremy couldn't see it that way.

Jill errored greatly a second time by not studying more about the effects of war on a person. By gaining such knowledge, she could have done a better job giving Jeremy the space that he needed rather than heap unrealistic expectations upon the situation. With all his might, Jeremy tried to hide these effects from his family because he didn't want to burden them. For her part, Jill knew that her baby boy wielded a strong spirit, soul, and body. In her eyes, he stood almost superhuman. She expected him, in time, to recover from his quandaries because she knew his strong character and tenacity. He never quit. She fully anticipated that, after a period of suffering, he would overcome all his torments. Much to her chagrin, Jeremy was simply human like everyone else. Consequently, the torments stubbornly persisted. She realized over time that she held a biasedly high regard for her son, a perception that Jeremy didn't really embody. She figured that he would come home from the war upset but that they could talk through it all, and he would conquer the issues since that was what they always did throughout his childhood.

In the past, Jeremy usually talked to Jill when dealing with something—but no longer. Not only did he refuse to talk with her about it, but he also got angry if she tried to connect with and console him. Only his brothers-in-arms had the right to discuss such sacred matters with him. No intruders from outside the brotherhood would be tolerated. Jill found herself in unfamiliar territory, no longer having a close relationship with her son. The situation wounded her deeply as if she too were somehow a casualty of war, another sacrifice upon the altar of freedom. She didn't know how to wrap her head around this new reality. She only knew that her son made it abundantly clear with a curt rebuke that she trespassed on prohibited ground. Jill didn't know how to respond.

No longer confiding in his mom, Jeremy turned to alcohol for solace and incessantly listened to dark songs. Silence and solitude became his refuge upon which darkness gladly encroached. Isolated by his guilt and self-condemnation, Jeremy became easy prey for torment and grief. There had always been strength in numbers, but Jeremy chose not to embrace this truth. He never wanted to cause someone else pain, so he chose to suffer alone rather than burden someone else with his demons. As a result, he drank too much and too often, fecklessly attempting to deal with and numb the physical and emotional pain himself. Still the valiant warrior, he futilely battled darkness with the bottle, trying to drown it in booze. Unfortunately, by using inadequate weaponry and tactics, Jeremy was losing this war in a devastating way. The anguish and the alcohol compelled him to behave obnoxiously and loudly. On one occasion, he passed out in the front yard. Seeing her patriotic soldier son lying in that state devastated Jill's soul, wrenched her gut, and tore her heart in two. At that juncture, she simply wanted to scoop up her baby boy and hold him lovingly as if it would ease away the torment.

Each time that Jeremy returned safely from war, Jill felt grateful, relieved, scared, worried, sad, heartbroken, and grieved all at the same time. Elated that he came home, she constantly wanted to embrace and comfort him and transfer upon herself the heavy darkness that he carried. She would gladly bear it for life if it resulted in happiness and relief for her baby boy. So thankful for his return, she could have kissed every inch of ground upon which he walked. Overjoyed to be in his presence, Jill's eyes drank in every moment of his image. She longed to reach into his inner being and connect with his soul. Tragically, she couldn't even get remotely close to her son emotionally because Jeremy simply wouldn't allow it.

She didn't know why and often wondered if he became distant to protect her from the deep pain. Perhaps cavernous guilt caused him to fear that she would recoil at what he did in combat. Jill couldn't understand how their lives unfolded this way. Her heart grieved for Jeremy since the day he got into the Army recruiter's car and said, "See ya later, Mom!" Despite all her hope, she now realized that *later* hadn't and wouldn't ever arrive. Her baby boy who left that day never came back and never would. He permanently changed into a troubled man having served his country valiantly in war. Jill's heart will grieve over this until her final breath. These things too were profound offerings upon the altar.

In rare moments, Jill saw glimpses of the pre-war Jeremy, her baby boy she missed so much. A fleeting smile, a hearty laugh, or a humorous joke from Jeremy graced the Smith family once in a great while, such a refreshing respite for Jill, which gave her hope. She recalled how he loved to hide by a wall in the house and roar loudly as she walked by, laughing emphatically at her startled response. Sometimes he gingerly pushed her shoulder with a finger just enough to throw her off balance. He loved joking around like that all the time. Sadly, all these fun family antics died for the most part after he came back from war. If she tried any of those tricks on him now, anxiety would throw him into a panic or fear would catapult him back to a distant battlefield. Life changed for them in so many ways.

Sometimes Jill just wanted to scream in despair at her son, "Hey! Remember me? Remember us? Remember how the family used to be? Come back to us, please!" In desperation, she made his favorite foods and spoke of the things he loved to do in a frantic attempt to trigger good memories and feelings of his childhood. All the while, she hoped in her heart that these actions reminded him of the love of his family, of his foundational upbringing, and most of all of the amazing person that God created him to be. She tried to encourage him by talking about how his bright future offered positive prospects. She pointed out to him that as a young man, he still had his whole life left to make of it what he wanted. Unfortunately, far too often, Jeremy just stared off into space and seemed frozen.

At times, Jill offered Jeremy advice on things he could do to feel better about life. Usually, it appeared as if he didn't hear her, like her words fell on deaf ears. For some reason, he pretended that they just couldn't reach him, or perhaps he simply had trouble believing in her encouraging words. One day, however, Jill told him that even though it seemed that he wasn't listening, she knew that he usually tried what she said. With a sheepish smile, Jeremy admitted with a chuckled, "You're right, Mom," surprised that she noticed. After he had stopped drinking, he confided in Jill that he was ready to straighten out his life by dealing with all his griefs. He said that no matter how much someone else wanted to keep him from drowning, he had to tread the water for himself. So, as he put it, he decided to start taking out the bricks from the bag that held him underwater.

Jeremy wanted to serve in the military until retirement. His family hoped that for him also. He felt edgy and useless when home on leave. His devotion to duty urged him to either train his soldiers thoroughly for combat or return to the war zone to protect and fight alongside his brothers. He toiled over this a lot. His entire family saw his deep dedication to duty and hoped that he could serve a full career in the Army, his ultimate dream. When it became apparent that he wouldn't have the opportunity to do this, Jill hoped that he could live for the Lord and build for himself a happy and rewarding life. She deeply hoped that he would somehow smoothly transition to civilian life despite the horrific effects of combat. As plan B, he wanted to become a state trooper once he got out of the Army. He loved justice, righteousness, and fairness. Unfortunately, his physical war wounds prevented him from realizing this dream as well, another sacrifice for the altar.

In reality, Jeremy didn't fully return from war in a sense. A part of him constantly remained on the battlefield. War continually churned within him. He fought too hard and long, as well as saw too many horrors. He tried to leave the war behind. God bless him, he tried. He fought hard every single day to do so. He drove countless miles, filled out a multitude of paperwork, and spent a myriad of hours at this VA facility and that VA center only to get the runaround. When he did have mental health appointments, he felt that the medical staff were detached, focusing only on red flags for which to hospitalize him as a danger to himself and others rather than genuinely trying to help him get better. Cynicism grew in his heart prompting Jeremy to distrust and not fully confide in the VA. He became guarded as to what he would say to them. To him, they became just another threat with which to contend.

Frustrated, Jeremy drank to cope. He earnestly tried to avoid self-medicating with alcohol. However, his brain injury affected his reasoning abilities and decision making. The unending nerve-damage pain from his leg injury tormented him constantly. He refused to take opioids, so his inevitable solution became booze. In reality, he may not have died on the battlefield, but the effects of war and inadequate treatment afterward seemed to slowly kill him just the same. When Jeremy physically returned from war, Jill let out a huge sigh of relief. When she finally saw him again in person she couldn't breathe. She thought, *It's over. We can go home and finally rest from this awful tribulation.* Little did she know that the war didn't end when the warrior came home. Another war on the home front merely began.

Every combat warrior sacrificed for our freedom. That sacrifice didn't end once they stepped off the plane to return home. Many had to fight daily to embrace civilian life and if wounded physically or emotionally, to fight for their promised care. The combat veteran's struggle would inevitably impact family and friends as well, adding further grief and guilt to the already heavy load that the warrior carried. Jill sincerely considered herself nobody special, just a mom of one of those warriors. As best she could, Jill served God in heaven who said in Exod 15:3, "The LORD is a warrior; the LORD is His name." She found peace in the fact that God was a combat veteran and that he too knew the fight just like her son Jeremy. Her prayer for all combat veterans and their families mirrored Oliver Wendell Holmes's sentiment that God would cause war's trumpet to cease and wrap the world in peace.

4

A Father's Double Portion

Sitting quietly next to Jill, Terry gazed upon his son lying there silently in what felt like a still, sterile room. Terry began to reminisce about the day when Jeremy left for boot camp at the young age of twenty. This reflection reminded him of when his dad, Leo Smith, joined the Army at the tender age of seventeen to fight in World War II. Leo, an intelligent young man, hailed from a family that valued faith and education in the small town of Benton, Kentucky. Having a good portion of the Bible committed to memory, he preached some and taught Sunday School. A phenomenal shooter, especially with the shotgun, Leo went to the shotgun national championship sometime after World War II and tied for first place. It came down to the two of them and neither missed their shots. Leo finally decided that enough was enough! He shot his final rounds haphazardly in the direction of the skeets and declared, "Let's go to the clubhouse!" As a young child, Terry watched people throw glass marbles off their porch while Leo shot each one without fail with a 22-caliber rifle. Undeniably talented with firearms, few people hunted with Leo because he always shot the birds first. Eventually, Marshall County shooting competitions asked Leo not to participate anymore because nobody could compete with him. Even when Leo opted to use an old single-shot 12-gauge shotgun with a 36-inch barrel and to stand farther back near the club house, he still won.

The oldest of five children, Leo's parents revered him most, much to the chagrin of his siblings, who complained that he always hailed as the favorite. Outgoing and somewhat flashy by nature, Leo cherished nice cars, sported fancy clothes, and loved attention from others. Confident and somewhat cocky, he sometimes offended others with a gauche, in-your-face attitude. Regardless, most people took a liking to him. An action-loving young man, he only liked fishing if the fish were vigorously biting. Otherwise, boredom prevailed. Jeremy was the same way.

At seventeen years old, Leo lied about his age to join the Army in 1943. Like so many other young men in the small towns and cities of the United States, he wanted to fight for and defend our country's freedom and liberty against the Nazi menace and Japanese imperialism. He entered the theater of war in 1944 during the Battle of Anzio in the Italian Campaign. Serving in the Infantry, he performed duty as a sniper because of his superior prowess with firearms. Numerous times, he looked at a man's face through the rifle scope and then snuffed out his life. A soldier who got things done no matter how difficult or grisly, he fought his way up the Italian peninsula.

Leo rose to the rank of SSG as he led a squad of soldiers in France and Germany. He and his comrades entered France as part of the Invasion of Normandy. While fighting in a French town, they exchanged fire with the enemy. As Leo stood against a building, bullets started going through his pant leg. Though he tried desperately, he couldn't get his limb back any further. A bullet finally pierced his leg. Another time, he got shot in the torso. In addition to this, a German grenade blew him out of a foxhole resulting in a head injury. After getting wounded a total of four times, he received the Purple Heart with three clusters. He also earned the Silver Star and the Bronze Star.

During a patrol through the German countryside. Leo's squad advanced on a farmhouse to clear it of enemy soldiers. They surrounded the structure and called for any civilians to identify themselves and come out. No one answered. When Leo kicked in the door, a snarling German Shepherd dog lunged at him. He quickly sprayed it with a hailstorm of bullets from his Thompson submachine gun. Down the hall, he noticed the commotion of bodies falling lifelessly to the floor. As Leo slowly made his way down the corridor, he came upon the still, blood-soaked, lead-riddled bodies of a mother and her infant child, an image that would haunt him for life. In 1946, he received an honorable discharge from the Army.

After the war, Leo earned a living as a highly skilled machinist. Married with children, he simply wanted to live a normal life, the American dream. Haunted by the horrors of his combat experience, however, he drank a lot of alcohol to ease his torment. Because he suffered from severe PTSD, his wife Genon placed him in a VA facility with the desperate hope that the medical staff there could nurture him to good mental and emotional health. Tragically, though, they forced Leo to leave after determining that he had no physical ailments. Labeling him as *just a drunk*, they resolutely declared that they needed the room for veterans who were actually sick.

Terry's family moved to Detroit, Michigan in the early 1960s. As a little boy, Terry watched the TV show *Combat* with his dad. The show depicted a squad of soldiers fighting its way across Europe. Leo pointed out to his son what was realistic and accurate and what wasn't. One morning, as Terry watched cartoons, Leo sat on the couch reading the newspaper. Terry asked his dad a question but got no response. Turning around, he looked at his dad and stared in horror as Leo convulsed from a seizure. The doctor concluded that scar tissue on the brain from one of his war wounds caused it. The doctor gave him phenobarbital to treat the epilepsy, but Leo typically sold the drug to buy alcohol. Whenever that memory of his dad emerged, it not only dampened Terry's eyes but also his heart. A good man and a brave patriot, Leo didn't deserve an outcome like that.

When Terry was about eight years old, his mom worked in the afternoons. Sometimes when Genon came home, she found Leo extremely intoxicated. At such times, he relived his combat experiences. In his mind, he no longer sat at home but drudged back in Europe fighting the war. Terry heard his dad yell out directives to his soldiers to do this and then to do that in order to get out of the harrowing situation in which they found themselves. The vision so real to Leo, he actually physically motioned ducking this way and dodging that way to avoid enemy fire.

Bearing guilt deep within his soul, Leo never forgave himself for things he did in the war. Ghoulish memories taunted him daily, such as the recollections of looking through the sniper scope, easing the trigger rearward, and seeing another human being's head snap back as his body fell lifelessly to the ground; or the stiff, cold stare of a mother and infant in a farmhouse inquisitively looking at him beseeching, "Why are we dead, Leo? What did we do to deserve this?" Who were these people? From where did they come? What would they have accomplished in life if not for Leo? These apparitions of recollection haunted him continually. At times, he just cried and cried and cried.

Having difficulty finding work in Kentucky, Leo moved his family to Evansville, Indiana for a new job which, unfortunately, he didn't hold on to long. Consequently, they moved back to Kentucky and lived with Terry's grandparents. Again, Leo found a job but didn't hold on to that one long either. They moved again, this time to Detroit, Michigan, where Genon got a job as a waitress in a hotel restaurant. Leo only held this job for six months. After that, he worked for a few weeks, then went unemployed for a month or so and then worked for another few weeks. This cycle went on indefinitely because of his heavy drinking. He drank profusely mostly to escape his haunting memories of the war. Back then, the system didn't offer grief counselors for help because no significant understanding of PTSD existed.

If a person severely suffered from PTSD to the point that it negatively impacted life, society considered that person a weak failure.

Shortly after moving to Detroit, Leo had his first seizure. Selling his seizure medication and buying alcohol, he always liked to have a big wad of money to flash around. When he did work, on payday he went to the bar and drank his money away. What he didn't spend, other patrons stole from him. One time he came home and passed out at the kitchen table with two ten-dollar bills sticking out of his shirt pocket. At the time, Terry only had one pair of shoes with worn out soles. So, he quietly and cautiously took one of the bills out of his dad's pocket. When Genon got home from work, Terry told her what he had done, gave her the money, and asked for a new pair of shoes. Genon replied, "Yeah and go back in the kitchen and get the other ten-dollar bill from your dad too."

Genon tried to help Leo dry out and quit drinking. She endured twenty years of grief dealing with Leo's alcoholic self-medication of PTSD. Finally fed up, she gave him one last chance; Leo tried to oblige her. Genon had a hidden bottle of whiskey from which she would give him little doses of alcohol here and there when he got really bad. Leo did really well for almost two weeks. Tragically, he found the whiskey bottle one day while the family went grocery shopping. Genon had just cleaned the apartment that morning. When they came home, they found Leo drunk as a skunk with the apartment ransacked in search of the booze. Unable to endure anymore, Genon took her children and moved back to Kentucky in 1966. At the age of nine, Terry looked back through the apartment door as he left and saw his dad sitting dejected at the kitchen table. Terry never saw his dad again, a sacrifice laid upon the altar of freedom.

In 1968, Genon divorced Leo and remarried. While at his paternal grandparents' house in 1969, Terry got to talk with his dad for a little bit on the phone. After that, the family lost all contact with and information about Leo. A decorated World War II veteran, Leo lived somewhere on the streets of Detroit withering away as a wino. After graduating from high school and earning some money, Terry went to Detroit looking for his dad. He did this a few times over the years but never had any luck finding Leo, who never carried identification and lingered in bad health. Somewhere on the filthy streets of skid row, the young man who had talent and promise, the soldier who displayed courage and valor died alone. This unceremonious event demonstrated the high cost of freedom's blessings.

Terry always loved his dad dearly. Even as a young child, he recognized that his dad suffered from haunting specters that came home with him from the war, making Leo a true war casualty. Terry possessed gratefulness in his heart that he got to know his dad before he became a fatality of war. Wishing that he could have known his dad better, Terry acknowledged that life sometimes required sacrifices to sustain freedom and liberty. Leo suffered greatly for his wife and children, for his extended family, for his friends, and for America. Terry cherished the memories of the few times that he and his dad went fishing and hunting together. Terry didn't harbor resentment toward his dad. Rather, he harbored sorrow for the torment that Leo suffered for others and for a nation. Under the umbrella of freedom and liberty resulting from Leo's sacrifice, Terry received a good upbringing from his grandparents, aunts, and uncles. His family inspired him to do well in life.

Terry completed school and became a journeyman tool and die maker. Even though he had his civilian livelihood established, he still wanted to serve in the military in some capacity. Much of Terry's family had done so. His paternal grandfather fought in World War I, his dad in World War II. He had an uncle who fought in Korea and other relatives who fought in Vietnam. Because many members of his family fought to keep America safe and free, he felt compelled to do the same. Therefore, in 1979 at the age of twenty-one, Terry joined the Army National Guard in order to serve readily if his country needed him. Terry ultimately served in the Guard for twelve years. He attended basic training and artillery forward observer school at Fort Sill, Oklahoma. About a year later, he seized the opportunity to go to officer candidate school at Fort Benning, Georgia and graduated as a second lieutenant. Returning to Fort Sill, he attended the artillery officer basic course.

Terry took his National Guard duty very seriously. Looking back upon this, he remembered staunchly believing that he needed to acquire for himself and bestow upon his soldiers as much skill and expertise as possible. He diligently instilled pride and a spirit of excellence into his soldiers by giving them challenging training. He wanted them to become truly professional soldiers especially because they served as a nuclear-capable unit handling special weapons. This reminiscence about training brought forth one of Terry's fondest memories when he taught his son, Jeremy, to shoot at the age of six. Terry put a coke can against an old building, handed Jeremy his Smith & Wesson .38 caliber pistol, and gave him a lesson in firearms. Jeremy then proceeded to shoot the can six times out of six from twenty feet away. Highly impressed, Terry marveled at his young son's accomplishment, despite the gun looming hugely in Jeremy's little hands. Terry proudly admired his son's determination to do the task well. Jeremy carried this attitude through much of his life.

Always fascinated with the military and an exceptionally good shot, Jeremy loved to shoot firearms. Terry trained his son to handle weapons and to shoot at a young age. He taught him about the potential danger and destructiveness of weapons when not handled correctly. Consequently, Jeremy knew early on what weapons could do and how to manage them. When given a firearm, he first checked to make sure that no round sat in the chamber. He never took anyone's word for it. In addition to his fondness for weapons, he loved to play army, spending hours with his G.I. Joes, tanks, military trucks, and toy guns.

Another memory emerged as Terry stared off into space with a slight smile invigorating his countenance. During one Halloween, Terry and Jeremy dressed up in military uniforms and went out trick-or-treating. Jeremy drove in his battery-operated Bigfoot truck adorned with chem lights while Terry walked. Eager and excited, Jeremy didn't want to stop trick-or-treating even though it wore out Terry, who thought to himself, *Surely that truck battery will run down soon!* Unfortunately for Terry, neither Jeremy nor the truck would quit.

Another time, when Jeremy was about ten years old, Terry bought a boat. Lacking safety chains for the trailer but anxious to get the boat in the water, Terry declared, "Come on, Jeremy. Let's go to Barren Lake and try the boat out!" After hooking the trailer to the truck, they cruised down Highway 100, all things well with the world. While crossing a bridge, the truck hit a bump. Terry looked in the rear-view mirror and saw the trailer and boat veering away. Pointing he yelled, "Oh no, Buddy. We got trouble!" Jeremy looked just in time to see the trailer hit a ditch and the boat shoot past them into a telephone pole. His eyes were as big and round as saucers. After turning around and pulling up to the boat, they encountered two old men who stared in disbelief. One of them declared, "I have been around for a long time and never seen anything like that!"

Later that day, Jeremy learned a grave lesson in life. As they had pulled out of the driveway to go to the lake, neither Terry nor Jeremy noticed that their dog Ginger got out and followed them. Ginger loved Jeremy so much that she just wanted to be with him. Of course, she couldn't keep up with the truck, which kept on going because neither occupant saw her. As she subsequently wandered on the highway, a car hit and killed her. Jeremy really loved Ginger and took the loss hard. Terry explained to him that pets didn't live forever and eventually died. That was just a reality of life. That day, Jeremy learned that life eventually separated us from our loved ones, so cherish the time that you had with them.

Because Terry grew up in Detroit, he learned to deal with adversity through the school of hard knocks. Terry worried that Jeremy wouldn't learn how to deal with adversity as a sensitive kid living in the county. Consequently, Terry began to deal sternly with his son when he reached the age of twelve. Terry surmised that if Jeremy learned to stand up to him, then he could face any situation that life threw his way. As a teenager, Jeremy didn't understand his dad's change in attitude. Later in life, he recognized and appreciated what his dad did, realizing that it must have been a tough thing for him to do.

At the age of twelve, Jeremy asked Terry why he served in the National Guard. Terry replied that his grandfather served in World War I, his father served in World War II, Uncle Jim fought in the Korean War, and that he had other uncles who fought in the Vietnam War. A myriad of Americans fought, and some died to keep this country free. Terry wanted to avail himself in case an enemy threatened the United States. It became a longstanding Smith family contribution to this nation to defend our freedom and liberty and sometimes that of other countries. Jeremy solemnly looked at his dad, nodded his head, and said that was a good reason.

Terry recalled the time when Jeremy learned how to drive. A nerve-racking experience, Terry sat in the passenger seat and instructed his son while he drove through town. As he pulled into a gas station, Jeremy approached the pump island rather fast and drew up almost on top of it. Scared to death, Terry thought they were going to take out the gas pumps. A big explosion played out in his mind. Rather, Jeremy sat there with a big smile on his face, completely pleased with himself for what he accomplished. He thought it proper to get as close to the gas pumps as possible. Jeremy's jubilation quickly evaporated when his dad erupted, reprimanding him for getting so close to the pumps. Terry bellowed out, "The island is for the gas pumps not for you to park your car on!"

Not sure of what he did wrong, young Jeremy looked at his dad in confusion. Terry then took a deep breath to calm himself and further explained, "You don't stand on the pump island itself when pumping gas. You leave room between the vehicle and the pump island for that." Throughout the years, they always had a good laugh over how he scared the heck out of his dad that day. Finally, the time came when Jeremy got his first vehicle. Terry paid twelve hundred dollars for an old two-tone pick-up truck, which Jeremy called *BLU*—big, loud, and ugly. Over time, Jeremy paid his dad back every penny even though Terry objected. However, the young man insisted.

When Jeremy reached the age of sixteen, Terry told him that even though *Smith* hailed as a common last name all around the world, Jeremy would fashion the repute of his last name by how he lived his life. His name would only be as good as he made it. Terry went on to say that a person's name is only as good as one's word and one's quality of character. Overall, their particular Smith family name brought respect because they didn't quit, did what they said they would do, and behaved honestly. Therefore, Jeremy should be proud of his last name and the family from which he came.

Jeremy took his dad's counsel to heart. He did whatever his parents asked of him because he respected them and their Smith name immensely. A no-nonsense person, Terry ensured a respectful and polite demeanor from his children. Jeremy dutifully complied. He had a good heart and always showed concern for the needs of others. If he could intervene and solve a problem, he generally did so.

After learning to play the bass, Jeremy then mastered the acoustic and electric guitar. He had a natural talent for it. He also liked to sing. During his senior year, he assisted with the school play by sitting on stage during intermission and entertaining the audience. He sang and played the guitar solo with great stage presence, performing the song *Simple Man* by Lynyrd Skynyrd. His deep, rich voice filled every crevasse of the auditorium. The music seemed a part of him. Terry and Jill watched in amazement, pride welling up in their hearts.

Upon graduating from high school, Jeremy got a job at Afni, Inc. in Bowling Green, Kentucky as an inbound customer resolution special-ist assisting callers with cellphone issues. Terry urged him to go to college while he still had good study habits. He cautioned Jeremy that the longer he waited to go to college the harder it would be. Jeremy acknowledged his dad's advice but recognized that he just wasn't ready for college. He rea-soned, "Dad, if I go to college at this point in my life, all I would be doing is wasting your money." During this time, 9/11 happened, which greatly upset Jeremy. He pondered for months what he wanted to do with his life and whether he should enlist in the Army. A few months later, he switched to an employer located in Franklin, Kentucky. He became a machine operator and then a line technician at Harman Becker Automotive Systems, making high-end speakers for cars. He spent this time in his life doing what most young people do—he earned his money and then went about spending it.

When the Iraq War started in March 2003, Jeremy decided to join the Army and discussed the notion with his dad. Terry actually tried to discour-age him from doing so in order to test his resolve about the matter. He said, "Oh, you don't want to join the military. You'll be out in the field in the mud, cold and uncomfortable, and away from home on your birthday stuck on guard duty somewhere." Jeremy didn't waver. Terry then tried to persuade his son to go into the Air Force to minimize his potential exposure to dan-ger. However, Jeremy would have none of it—Army all the way! As a small child, he looked up to Terry as he left the house in his military uniform for Army National Guard duty. Terry had bought him an outfit that resembled a military uniform. Jeremy loved it and wore it to threads. Nothing but the Army would do, so he enlisted in April 2003.

He then spent the summer with his friends, playing music and video games, riding around in trucks, driving fast, and probably drinking a few beers along the way, stuff that young people did in America. Jeremy had a white Chevy S10 Extreme pickup truck with all the extras like tuned headers and dual exhaust pipes. He called it the White Streak. He took time to live a little bit by having a season of fun and making good memories with his friends before he entered the Army. When Jeremy signed up, he weighed 305 pounds and had to get down to 255 by August. When the time came, he met the Army height/weight standards by two pounds, losing all that weight in less than four months, a proud achievement in his life. At the age of twenty, Jeremy eagerly went to basic training with an inner peace about the whole thing, even though Jill grieved over his leaving. Charged with excitement and resolve, he stepped out on his own as an adult focused on what he wanted to do in life, establishing concise personal goals. He eagerly moved ahead to confront the challenges that faced him. Jeremy had his mind in the right place and met the requirements to join the Army, which began his new journey. Impressed and proud of Jeremy, the recruiters applauded his efforts and accomplishments.

Right before Jeremy left for basic training, his S10 started running roughly. Terry suspected that the engine threw a rod. Unhappy and unable to do anything about it at the time, Jeremy decided to fix his truck when he came back on leave after basic training. While Jeremy trained at Fort Leonard Wood, Missouri, his parents decided to get the S10 fixed. After having a mechanic look at it, they rejoiced to find out that it only needed a new distributor, a two-hundred-dollar repair. When Jeremy came home on his first leave, he languished over his truck. Terry suggested that he start it up to see how it sounded. Upon doing so, the S10 ran perfectly. Looking at his parents with an ear-to-ear grin, Jeremy exclaimed, "What did you do? What did you do, Dad? What did you do?" Elated, he and the White Streak sped off into the wind.

Jeremy muscled through basic and advanced individual training while battling pneumonia and losing another seventy pounds in the process. His appearance and demeanor changed so much that his parents hardly recognized him. He tackled any challenge that came his way and never whined. To Terry, his son became like a military robot. He stood at-ease constantly, got up early in the morning to polish his boots, did PT every day, and called everybody *sir* or *ma'am*. He continually displayed military bearing in overload. Jeremy poured his heart and soul into being the best soldier that he could. Consequently, he found it difficult to relax and shift gears to fit in a civilian environment. After thirty days of leave just prior to departing for assignment at Fort Wainwright, Alaska in January 2004, he began to relax allowing glimpses of the old Jeremy to emerge.

Jeremy didn't have any cold weather gear, so Terry gave him an old big heavy coat he had since living in Michigan years ago. Not wanting to take something that his dad might need, Jeremy objected. Terry countered, "You may not need it here, but you will definitely need it when you step off the plane in Alaska. When it's forty below zero, you'll be glad you have it. You won't have anything like this to keep you warm until the Army issues it to you up there." Jeremy abdicated and put on the coat. It swallowed him up because he had lost so much weight. Consequently, his comrades at his new duty station teased him.

Jeremy did his first tour of duty assigned to the 562nd Engineer Company under the 172nd Stryker Brigade Combat Team. He found himself in a solid, professional unit with competent leadership. They conducted a lot of urban assault training in anticipation of deployment to Iraq. Jeremy excelled in his duties and training. When a SGT told him to do something, he took it to heart, did it with fervor to the best of his ability, and considered failure unacceptable. The SGTs learned quickly that they had to watch what they said to him in jest because he took it as a serious order. As a young soldier, they put him in charge of running the opposition forces (OPFOR) during training exercises. At times, the battalion deemed his squad the best during field maneuvers. Jeremy enjoyed excelling in his military duties and took training seriously to become the most effective soldier possible. He wanted to give the best training plausible to his soldiers to enhance their safety and survival on the battlefield. This would soon pay big dividends.

About a year-and-a-half later, the unit deployed to Iraq in August 2005, first going to Kuwait for about three weeks to acclimate since they came from an extremely cold environment. They went from daily highs of sixty-five degrees to that of 105. Their bodies had to develop more pores and sweat glands to accommodate the hotter climate. They then moved from there to an FOB in Mosul, Iraq. Terry and Jill didn't hear from him for a couple of months. Shortly after arriving in the theater of war, Jeremy advanced to the rank of SGT. After four months of combat, he went home in December on leave. Jeremy sat in an easy chair in the living room across from the Christmas tree and stared incessantly at it as the twenty-two-year-old man cried in appreciation for freedom, liberty, and a blessed home. With tear-soaked words, he declared, "I am so glad to be home! I thought I would never see another Christmas. I thought that I would never be home again." He rambled like this for the longest time. It was the first instance when he had shown an emotion other than subdued anger. Terry discerned that his son saw tough things in combat that affected his very persona.

After Christmas leave, Jeremy rejoined his unit in Iraq. During this deployment, some young teenagers pummeled Jeremy and his squad with bottles, rocks, and various debris from atop a mud building. Not wanting to hurt the youngsters, they took no retaliatory action. Suddenly a twenty-five-pound block slammed Jeremy on the helmet. Any other man would have suffered a broken neck. Jeremy staggered and then fell but got back up. Although he suffered a concussion, he joked about bringing the block back to the states as a trophy. The Army extended his unit's deployment from a twelve to a sixteen-month tour to help stabilize conditions in Baghdad. During the fall of 2006, Jeremy took part in combat operations in Fallujah, conducting mostly infantry type missions in an effort to clear out insurgents from that province.

While assigned to the 562nd, Jeremy looked up to three of his fellow soldiers who greatly inspired him. SPC Jeremiah Boehmer and SGT Christopher Morningstar died from an IED blast on February 5, 2006, in Husayniyah. It was Superbowl Sunday. This devastated Jeremy, who for years to come couldn't watch football because it reminded him of the death of these two brothers-in-arms whom he revered as heroes. He began to loathe all Iraqi people, wondering why they didn't just kill them all and then go home. Another icon to Jeremy, SSG Bryan Luckey explained to him that not all Iraqis are violent radical extremists. He reasoned that most were ordinary people like Jeremy and he. They had families whom they loved, livelihoods, and just wanted peace and happiness as did most people in the world. Jeremy never heard SSG Luckey say a bad word about anything. His wisdom put Jeremy's mind in the proper context. SSG Luckey died June 29, 2006, in Mosul, from the bullet of an enemy combatant sniper that struck him in the head. Jeremy felt a huge sense of loss when these three men died. They had helped him become a better person and a better soldier. He wrote and read the eulogy for SSG Luckey at his farewell ceremony in Iraq. It was the hardest thing that he ever had to do in his life.

Jeremy saw a lot of things in war that he couldn't do anything about. This tormented him deeply. He struggled with lots of ghosts, things for which he couldn't forgive himself or see how others could forgive him. He wrestled with regret, pondering in hindsight that if he did this instead of that, things would have turned out better. Terry tried to impress upon his son that in the heat of battle, a person only had a split second to make a decision and react to a dangerous situation when lives hung in the balance. He had to act instantly to protect the lives of his brothers. Terry forewarned Jeremy before he deployed to Iraq that he would experience things in war that would bother him for life. Regardless, he would only have one momentary chance in many cases to protect his comrades and himself. Terry tried to prepare his son to forgive himself for decisions and actions that wouldn't turn out so well. Despite all this, Jeremy ultimately couldn't forgive himself for participating in the hell of war.

Upon Jeremy's return from sixteen months in Iraq, his countenance displayed a hollow, distant look. He drank alcohol a lot and seemed to have a heavy weight bearing down upon his shoulders. As Jeremy's service continued, the cast on his demeanor greatly resembled that of his grandfather Leo. They paralleled each other. This concerned and grieved Terry because his dad was, indeed, a casualty of World War II. He just made it home for a while before he died. Terry recognized that combat took a grave toll on Jeremy as well. However, he never pushed him to talk about what he experienced. Terry figured that if Jeremy wanted him to know, he would tell him. Terry did make sure that his son knew that he was definitely there for him if he wanted to talk about anything.

While home on leave, Terry and Jeremy went to Bowling Green, about twenty-five miles north of Franklin. As they approached each overpass, Jeremy nervously strained to observe if anyone stood upon it with nefarious intentions. Terry asked, "What are you doing, Son?"

Visibly shaken, Jeremy proclaimed, "That's where they attack us from, Dad! That's where they attack us! I was just making sure that no one was up there to hurt us."

Terry tried to reassure his son, "This is Kentucky. There's nobody hiding on the overpass to attack us."

Jeremy shot back, "I just want to make sure, Dad." As of yet, Jeremy couldn't shut off his heightened awareness of danger that he developed for survival in a combat environment. No longer the robot soldier, Jeremy possessed the demeanor of one who had feared for his life repeatedly, a person who had faced perils and prevailed physically but had a scarred psyche. When they went out to public places, Jeremy's mind would process the situation and the surroundings, assessing the people there to determine the presence of threats. At this point in his life, Jeremy constantly possessed a combat frame of mind, always serious and on guard, only able to relax somewhat when at home in the house of his childhood. Knowing that his son could face combat again, Terry actually took some comfort with Jeremy's elevated situational awareness.

After a couple weeks at home, Jeremy went out a few times with some of his old friends but didn't stay out long with them. His friends couldn't appreciate what Jeremy had experienced in combat and joked about his deportment. Jeremy marveled in dismay at their finite cognizance of the world, most of them never having ventured far from their hometown. In response to a few of his friends mocking him, Jeremy sternly admonished them for their ignorance of the world beyond their little rural county, for never having gone anywhere, and never aspiring to do anything meaningful with their lives. Proud of his son, Terry lamented the naivety of Jeremy's friends. Jeremy put his life on the line, saw his comrades perish in battle, and endured hardship to defend the liberties, freedoms, and blessings of his friends. It greatly disappointed him that they lacked insight and appreciation for what he and his military brothers did for them and their families. From this time on, Jeremy's group of friends no longer consisted of civilians, but of those affiliated with the military who had an understanding of that life.

Shortly after Jeremy returned to Fort Wainwright, the Army deactivated the 172nd Stryker Brigade, redesignating and redistributing all its subordinate units throughout the Army. As a result, Jeremy ventured to his new unit, Company A, Special Troops Battalion, 101st Airborne Division located at Fort Campbell, Kentucky. Jeremy had hoped that one day he would be stationed at Fort Campbell. He chose to live at home and make the eighty-minute drive twice daily. At this point in his life, he had a heaviness in his heart because of what he experienced in combat. Living at home provided some comfort. The first thing he did when he arrived to live at home again was to plop down on the trap and take a long nap. Every night, Jill had dinner waiting for him when he rolled in around seven in the evening, ravenous as he hit the front door. This gave him stability and a small sense of well-being. Jeremy especially felt safe around his dad, a former military man who was never far from a loaded weapon. Jeremy, himself, slept with a loaded .44 Magnum, a privilege not afforded to him in the barracks at Fort Campbell. He couldn't sleep otherwise.

As the months went by, Jeremy, desiring a place of his own, bought a small house surrounded by farmland near Dawson Springs, Kentucky, north of Fort Campbell. Terry once told him, "Son, they're making all kinds of stuff, but they're not making any more land. If you have the money and the inclination, you may want to buy some for yourself." Jeremy took that to heart. Wanting to surprise his parents, he kept it to himself. He went out and got a realtor on his own, went house-hunting, got a loan, and then bought a house. After closing on the real estate contract, he declared with a wide grin, "Hey Mom and Dad, I bought a house. Want to see it?" Amazed and proud of their son, they gladly obliged. Jeremy never wanted to burden other people, least of all his parents. After a season of living at home, he moved out to stand again on his own two feet. He always strove for self-sufficiency, never wanting help from anyone else, but would always be the first to assist others. He never accepted the fact that there came a time in everyone's life to lean on others for support, in addition to standing on one's own.

In March 2008, Jeremy left for another combat deployment, this time in Afghanistan. Upon his return home, he seemed more distant, withdrawn, and harder to reach, obviously affected and conflicted by his experiences. When danger threatened his comrades and him, Jeremy challenged it with extreme intensity and reckless abandon. This constant elevated level of stress took a heavy toll upon his psyche. He drank alcohol even more and wouldn't let people near him physically. He complained that they were in his space. He dated a young lady named Shawna. As fireworks ignited at a football game, he grabbed her and threw her to the ground covering her protectively. Upon realizing that they weren't in a combat situation, Jeremy got up greatly embarrassed, while Shawna was greatly disturbed by his behavior.

After his second Afghanistan deployment in June 2010, where he got blown up, he suffered from traumatic brain injury (TBI). He used to be extremely sharp and could process things well, making quick, sound decisions. However, when enemy combatants fired depleted uranium rounds from a recoilless rifle into their Stryker vehicle, the impact thumped and dazed Jeremy and his comrades. In addition, the round completely severed the leg of the soldier sitting across from Jeremy and greatly damaged Jeremy's leg as well. As his leg clung to his body by shredded skin and tissue, he ensured that all the injured soldiers in the vehicle put their tourniquets on correctly.

After this incident, Jeremy struggled to make decisions and to cope with issues in life as his ability to manage stressful things diminished. With depleted uranium shrapnel in his body, he suffered constant pain from his injured leg, which made him moodier. From then on, Terry only saw glimpses of his son as he knew him before joining the Army. On rare occasions, Jeremy behaved like his old self, witty and easy going. But most of the time, he was a person severely affected by the traumas of war. If he wanted to be left alone, Terry obliged him. Jeremy continued to enjoy shooting weapons. It was one of the few things he continued to be good at and on which he could focus. It gave him a sense of control in his out-of-control life. He had a certain tree at his house that he used as a target, which he referred to as his *shootin' tree.*

Jeremy finally reached a point where he couldn't perform his military duties anymore. He couldn't do PT and consequently gained a lot of weight. He couldn't fit in a uniform anymore or put a boot on over his shot-up leg. TBI diminished his mental capacity causing extreme difficulty dealing with everyday issues. He received a medical discharge on November 26, 2013, with 90 percent disability. He carried enormous guilt because his dad had to see him emotionally broken by the hellacious horrors of combat. Terry already went through this with his own dad. Now he had to relive it with his son. This extraordinary grief heaped upon Terry devastated Jeremy internally, who felt awful about it and flailed about powerlessly to change the situation, incapable of overcoming the torment that roiled inside him. Observing the negative impact that this added to his dad's life compounded the pain and guilt that Jeremy felt.

Terry served his country in peacetime, sacrificing his time and effort in the National Guard. He missed out on a good relationship with his dad and now had to witness PTSD devour his son. It was tough for Terry to see the stark parallel between his dad's behavior and that of Jeremy's. Tragically, he could do nothing about both situations. This was Terry's cross to bear for the sake of freedom and liberty, for the sake of all Americans.

If Jeremy could have stayed in the Army for life, he would have done so. Regrettably, he had to accept a discharge. Consequently, he worked in a gun shop for a while. He knew everything about every kind of weapon. Sadly, that job didn't work out for him. After that, he couldn't muster the ambition to get and hold another job and eventually moved back in with his parents. Terry discerned that Jeremy dealt with a lot of hard things and struggled to cope with himself and with life. He encased himself inside a big shell. After living with his parents again for about a year, the former Jeremy began to peak out of the shell showing improvement.

Jeremy found solace in playing music. He hooked up with three young musicians to form a band. The music and the camaraderie began to mend his soul. Unfortunately, at one of the practices, the dog of one of the other musicians startled Jeremy, engulfing him in a quagmire of negative feelings. Fear, anger, and hostility flooded his being and catapulted him back to the battlefield on which he fought years ago. Jeremy reasoned to himself that he was safe and secure in Kentucky. Nevertheless, angst refused to release him. Unrelenting, it pummeled him with a sense of impending doom, danger, and fear of death. Jeremy stood there shaking uncontrollably, a frightened look smothering his countenance. Using every ounce of strength within himself, he struggled for composure, which he eventually regained.

As a result of this episode, the rest of the band members branded Jeremy as unhinged and dangerous. They summarily cut him out of the band, refused to speak to him, and had nothing to do with him anymore. Unaware of their perceptions and feelings resulting from the episode with the dog, Jeremy didn't know why they suddenly rejected him. This added to the feelings of guilt and inadequacy that taunted him daily and ripped apart the mending seams of his soul.

Jeremy began to smoke marijuana to manage the intense pain inflicted upon him from nerve damage in his wounded leg. It subdued the pain better than any prescribed medication or alcohol. Not raised by his parents to be a drug user, guilt pelted him daily. However, he just couldn't bear the excruciating pain anymore. He had to find relief. He got to the point where he felt that he had no room or outlets to cope with his problems. Terry agonized over watching his son's life spin out of control just as his father's did because of combat in World War II. The similarities between their two lives were heart-rending.

5

A Sister's Sorrow and Solace

Leah sat with her parents, Terry and Jill, with great consternation for the well-being of her brother Jeremy. Not the typical older brother, he didn't fight much with his little sister, played well with her, and loved her dearly. Almost five years older than she, he often included her in whatever he did, whether playing G.I. Joes versus her Barbies or racing cars out in the back-yard. They often jumped on the trampoline or played video games together daily. Reminiscing about their childhood, Leah recalled that her big brother stood by her always. He often made her laugh by making impressions or telling jokes. When she played dress-up with her mom's clothes, he also adorned himself with mom's attire in a silly way to get a laugh. He continu-ally watched over and protected her.

When the Smith family moved to Kentucky, Leah, about the age of four, didn't want to leave Indiana. By nature, she refused to embrace change. She had always called the old house their home and wanted to keep it that way. The old neighborhood cradled all their childhood friends. Why change any of that? Jeremy, on the other hand, exploded with exuberance when the Smith family vehicle crossed over into Simpson County, Kentucky. Leah glowered at his celebration, one of her earliest memories of her older brother. Bullied at school in Indiana, the other kids teased him for his strong-willed antics. If he wanted to wear a full-length camouflage outfit with boots instead of shorts in one-hundred-degree weather, then he did exactly that, despite the jeering from others. Kentucky offered a fresh start for him regardless of Leah's objections.

Leah eventually settled into her new surroundings and called the little house on the quiet country lane home. She had fond memories of jump-ing on the trampoline for hours with Jeremy. Then, they lay down on the bouncy canvas, looked up at the sky, and just talked. In the evening, they star-gazed incessantly and talked about whatever. This constituted her favorite memories with her brother. As little kids, she lay on his back as he lay on his stomach, often times, falling asleep in that manner. When their parents had a heated argument, Jeremy took Leah into her room, sat on a beanbag chair in her closet with her, and told her stories to take her mind off their fighting parents. He always protected her, always made sure that she was okay. As they got older, Jeremy drove her to middle school in his truck. She thought him the coolest for driving his own truck as a high schooler. He often took her for drives around the countryside at night. They had a usual place on a bridge over a creek where they stopped and just talked about anything and everything. Out for drives late at night, they enjoyed their favorite music. Leah couldn't recall a single bad memory about her brother. Without a doubt, he hailed as her best friend with whom she could talk about anything. Even though she purposely got him in trouble when she was in an ill mood, he never reciprocated. Without fail, he always looked out for and protected her. Despite their age difference, Jeremy always included Leah in the things that he did with his friends.

Her only sibling, Jeremy knew the very foundation of Leah's upbringing that formed her into the person she became. She shared that common ground with no other. If she got mad at Mom or Dad, Jeremy always gave her a sympathetic ear. He had the ability to rationalize things and sooth her angst. Always holding a special place in her heart, he constantly encouraged her and lifted her spirit. After Jeremy joined the Army, she abruptly lost all that. When Leah first heard that Jeremy enlisted, she brimmed with extreme pride. She got an Army keychain from a recruiter and proudly put her keys on it. She still had that keychain today and refused to part with it. Anything patriotic gave her a great sense of satisfaction within her soul. Life now bittersweet, she spent her days sad but proud.

Jeremy left for basic training when Leah was fifteen years old. She felt as if she had lost her best friend. Absent for most of her teenage years, her life went from having him there every day to his complete absence, one extreme to the other. Suddenly, Leah became an only child during her adolescence. She remembered going to his military graduation and not even recognizing him. He transformed from a pudgy kid to a lean, muscular young man. The weight loss, coupled with his newly acquired military bearing, made him seem like a whole different person. He changed so much that Leah didn't feel as if Jeremy was the same brother with whom she grew up. A bit shocked, she found it difficult to talk to him because he seemed a complete stranger. She now felt a profound sense of abandonment by her big brother, her best friend since infancy. As a result, she withdrew from him in her teenage years. Irregardless, when he came home on leave, he took her out back and taught her self-defense. He also taught her how to handle and shoot guns, still very much her protector.

After basic training, Jeremy came back noticeably confident. He was skinny with muscles. An overweight kid most of his life, he now stood in front of the mirror admiring his new physique, an event that Leah snickered at because it was so unbecoming of the brother with whom she went through childhood. No longer laid back and relaxed, he walked about with a firm deportment, always speaking matter-of-factly. She missed joking around with her happy-go-lucky big brother that she enjoyed during their youth. Leah didn't know quite how to interact with this new more serious Jeremy. She missed the loving, kind bubble of emotion who never hesitated to give out hugs. Disorganized while growing up, he usually had a messy room. After basic training, everything had its place and PT had precedence in the wee hours of the morning. Afterward, he took his guitar into Leah's room, plopped on the bed, sang, and played with a resolute grin on his face. He ignored her pleas to leave and let her continue to sleep, as he insisted that the time had come for everyone to get up and go forth into this glorious day.

He let out a vigorous *hoowah!* to everything. He demonstrated great excitement for everything he did no matter how menial the task. This made Leah uneasy around him because she was not used to this kind of Jeremy and didn't yet know how to take him and interact with him. She felt that she, herself, walked on eggshells around a drill SGT, especially when he disagreed with her on something. Immediately, the knife hand came out accompanied by an admonishment. In addition, Leah felt pushed out of the way. She had a positive experience in high school where everyone liked her. She had lots of friends there and at church. Jeremy's experience had unfolded quite differently. Overweight with acne, he got teased a lot and had to study arduously to achieve good grades. At that time, Leah relished her position in the family as the golden child. Then Jeremy went into the Army and instantly became a hero, serving and sacrificing for the country. In light of that, Leah got moved to the side. Her accomplishments didn't seem to matter as much compared to Jeremy's military service. When he called home from overseas, the duration of the phone call was limited, so only Terry and Jill got to talk. Leah sat silently in the background feeling small compared to his valiant service in war. As a result, she only wrote him a couple of letters while he fought in Iraq.

After his first combat deployment, he came home on leave. While he lingered in the bathroom, Leah hid to scare him. They always found humor and laughter in scaring each other in this manner. As he emerged, Leah jumped out and frightened him. Within seconds, he pinned her to the wall with her feet dangling. As he glared at her with dark eyes, his hand tightened around her neck. She struggled to breath and desperately pleaded in horror, "Jeremy! Stop! It's me, Leah!"

When he realized the situation, he scolded his sister harshly. Putting her down, he angrily yelled, "Don't ever do that again!" From then on, things changed even more. She used to do random things like go into his room in the morning, run, jump on his bed, and wake him up. Sadly, such antics occurred no more. When Jeremy came home, they tried to pick up where they left off for the most part. Leah attempted to gingerly joke around with him despite his rigid demeanor and short temper. Growing up, he was a gentle, caring mama's boy who wore his feelings out on his sleeve and cried at times. After joining the military, that particular Jeremy ceased to exist. He refused to tolerate weak emotional displays.

When he came home on leave after serving in combat, however, they still went out on night rides through the countryside and talked. He tried to share his experience in combat and how he considered himself a monster, crying at times, as he revealed deep emotional pain. Taken aback at his candid feelings, Leah quietly listened and tried to console and reason with him. Surprised by his passionate cries for understanding and absolution, she had no idea that such turmoil roiled inside her brother. Betraying his own stoic emotive code, Jeremy got drunk and released his emotions to his sister, confiding in her his deepest torments.

Because of his short temper and anger tendency, Leah sadly withdrew further from him. In addition, she believed that some emotional distance would make it easier to handle the situation should he get injured in combat. As it turned out, detaching herself didn't help. The news from her dad in 2010 that Jeremy got severely wounded in Afghanistan devastated her, compelling her to immediately leave work that fateful day. She now regretted distancing herself from her brother all those years. Consequently, she arrived first to visit him at Walter Reed National Military Medical Center in Maryland.

During the years leading up to that dreadful event, when he came home on leave after combat, they still had their talks, where Jeremy mostly vented and leaned on Leah for support. Certain instances of killing other human beings in combat conflicted with his morals, especially women and children. He thought, *How could God forgive me, I'm a monster for killing.* He had killed a woman and a child resulting from threatening situations against his unit. He felt that his family couldn't fully appreciate the horrors through which he went. When Leah tried to reason with him, he retorted that she had no idea because she hadn't experienced it. Jeremy convinced himself that God couldn't love him because of what he did in war. He grappled greatly with this mental battle of self-condemnation.

Jeremy struggled with depression and withdrew from his family. Leah sent him encouraging songs, talked about positive things, and tried to point him toward God. She also attempted to divert his attention by talking about challenges that she had in life. Jeremy insisted that he still remained strong in his faith and that he wasn't condemned. However, whenever he got drunk, he always lamented over the same issues, having been ordered to kill women and even a child who posed threats to U.S. forces. Although justified, he felt like a monster because of it. He also lamented over collateral damage to innocent civilians due to the chaos of combat.

Normally rigid and reserved with a controlled deportment, Jeremy wept and bemoaned constantly over these things on their night drives and subsequent conversations while drunk. These vulnerable moments of seeing her hero brother like this shocked and saddened Leah. As a civilian, she didn't realize what combat veterans actually went through. She visualized them over there, fighting, keeping us safe, and doing their job. Unfortunately, she initially didn't step back and think about what they actually went through or how they could mentally deal with the experience of war.

Upon returning from combat, Jeremy wasn't so gung-ho about every little thing anymore. The way that he folded his clothes became insignificant. Leah took him to a school basketball game where he acted extremely nervous and edgy. He admired the cheerleaders not for their beauty but because they were the first uniformed outfit working together as a team that he saw since he came home. This sight made him feel comfortable. He insisted on sitting with his back to the wall so he could survey their entire surroundings for threats. When they went out to eat at a restaurant, he insisted on sitting at the table in a position where he could see everything, constantly surveying and evaluating.

Ill-tempered, he argued his point of view to the bitter end when having disputes with his sister. At first, sharing the bathroom again with her brother proved a tough adjustment. The only child in the house for years, Leah leisurely readied herself in the bathroom in the morning, agitated by Jeremy's complaints that she took too long. He couldn't understand why she took more than fifteen minutes especially when her lingering got in his way. A mouthy little teenager at the time, an irritated Leah responded with a snotty rebuke. In reply, Jeremy lurched toward her reprimanding Leah's selfishness. At such times, she just wanted to throttle her big brother for encroaching on her domain. Afterall, he was the one who left home years ago and now had reemerged.

Despite these spats, they got along for the most part. Leah enjoyed sitting back and listening to Jeremy, a natural anecdotist, tell stories that made people laugh or find joy with the small things in life. Growing up, Leah considered her brother a big, kind, loving teddy bear. After he came back from combat, Leah saw him as a bit scary and didn't know how to approach him. He got angry quickly, especially when he drank. His eyes and his walk seemed altogether different. His loving look became a cold stare emphasizing young eyes that had aged prematurely due to extreme stress and grief.

After the Army discharged Jeremy in 2013, he lectured Leah about the poor judgments and decisions she had made in life. It pained him to see his little sister struggle as a single mom when she had so much potential. She retorted that what occurred had occurred and couldn't change, so no benefit harping on it. Despite his disappointment in how she had lived her life during young adulthood, he told her that he still loved her most. She would forever be his favorite person. Because Leah had to work so much to make ends meet, the times that they spent together at family gatherings now became few and far between. Jeremy seemed dejected when she missed events like his birthday. Watching her brother battle to regain his life from PTSD made her own struggle in life all the more troubling. She found it difficult to bear the fact that her absence from his life caused him to grieve more.

As a retired disabled combat veteran on medication, Jeremy's faculties were dulled, exemplified by slurred speech and lethargic demeanor. He hated living that way. This ignited a deep sympathy in Leah for her brother. Despite her circumstances in life, she knew that now she had to step up and help take care of him as best she could. She bought him things when he needed them. She had him over to her apartment to feed him a nice dinner and to watch movies. She gave him advice to help him deal with his issues. The past few years, her big brother, who had protected and watched over her all her life, now needed that in return. She made sure that she was there to support him during major crises that came up in his shattered life despite her own challenges and shortcomings. As a single mom with two kids at the age of twenty-five, she personally knew the challenging impact and turmoil that poor decisions caused in one's life. Consequently, she empathized with Jeremy when he made poor decisions in trying to deal with PTSD. Not too long ago, Jeremy confided in her that he was just so extremely depressed, and life seemed impossibly hard. She encouraged him to set goals and take life one day at a time. She encouraged him, as a valiant warrior, to fight and survive until the age of thirty-five and then forty, then to evaluate the quality of his life at each of these milestones. He took that to heart.

In 2017, Leah married a musician and moved near Nashville, Tennessee. She visited Franklin, Kentucky on weekends when she could. In the spring of 2018, she and her husband rented a cabin on a lake and invited Jeremy for the weekend. She told him not to bring alcohol on account of her children. Jeremy went and found it a refreshing experience that helped him decompress. She arranged for the entire family to have professional photographs taken that Mother's Day. She also spent the 4th of July holiday with the Smith family. Because of his military service and PTSD, Jeremy didn't notice Leah's transition from a mouthy adolescent to a responsible adult. In those last few months, he marveled at her maturity and success as a mother and wife and had immeasurable pride in his little sister.

Now living sixty miles apart, they spent their days sending each other funny texts or memes. At this juncture, Leah only made it up to Franklin about twice a month to see her parents and brother. Striving to remain sober, Jeremy as of late had been acting like the brother with whom she grew up. It refreshed her soul to see his reemergence. Unaware of the fateful episode that August 2018 held in store, the Smith family relished these events where they spent time together with a rejuvenating Jeremy.

6

Family and Friends

Kelly Pierce, Terry's cousin, sat in the crowded room overwhelmed by the outpouring of love and support. She marveled at the dozens of current and former soldiers, Jeremy's brothers-in-arms, who traveled from all over the country, even one from Alaska, to be at his side in his time of need. She gazed upon Jeremy lying there quietly. A look of peaceful slumber now replaced the years of restless sleep. Although he was her second cousin, she always referred to him as her *baby boy*. Jill and Terry welcomed the endearing affection. Kelly thought back to 1983 when Grandmother Smith informed her that Terry and Jill became expectant parents. Jill gave birth to Jeremy Doyle Smith in August of that year. Baby Jeremy instantly won over Kelly's heart with his sparkling eyes, infectious smile, ginger red hair, and happy demeanor.

Terry and his family lived in Indianapolis, so Kelly kept in touch with phone calls and visits. When she called, a young Jeremy always answered the phone, "Smith residence." Without fail, he said *yes ma'am* and *no ma'am* and referred to his parents as *Mr. and Mrs. Smith*. Kelly admired his level of politeness and respect, rare virtues for a boy so young. As Jeremy grew, his list of amazing qualities also increased. He stayed over at Kelly's house a fair amount of time throughout the years. She had a special bond with him. Everyone who knew this bighearted young man had a special bond with him.

Jeremy, the embodiment of live entertainment and epitome of fun times, flourished when around a crowd. Several other members of the extended family possessed musical and singing talent. However, only Jeremy naturally thrived when entertaining a group of people. He just stood head and shoulders above everyone else in this respect. He could go anywhere with his guitar playing, singing, and comedy and make everyone feel good.

With his talent, he even wrote a song specifically for Kelly. He never wrote it down but sang it to her verbally. Since then, it dwelt in her heart as one of her greatest treasures of life.

The extended Smith family always celebrated Halloween with a fervor, zealously dressing in costume each year as they got together for a party. Kelly recalled her favorite year when Jeremy dressed up as Miss Piggy. After he pulled into the drive in his Corvette, he stepped out wearing a bright pink dress with two exceptionally large balloons stuffed into the bosom. When he came walking through the house, Kelly laughed so hard that she cried and could hardly breathe. That same year, Terry dressed up like Lady Gaga complete with wig, shoes, and the works. Superman made an appearance, along with Harley Quinn and Poison Ivy. At two PM everyone went to the road and waved to the passersby. With joy and laughter, cars honked, and people waved back as they drove past. That day, Jeremy's rendition of Miss Piggy took the prize.

That particular year, almost everyone spent the night at Kelly's home. As family and friends strewed themselves all over the house wherever they could find a place to sleep, several girls stayed in the master bedroom. Early the next morning, Jeremy banged on the door humorously pleading, "I want to sleep in the girls' room too!" As someone opened the door, he busted in and made a dive onto the middle of the bed where Kelly and a couple others lay. Kelly yelped in startled fright, convinced that the bed would disintegrate the moment Jeremy landed on it. The bed having endured, Jeremy proceeded to give Marianne a rejuvenating foot rub, while Kim grimaced that all she got from him was her toes set on fire the night before.

Kelly then recalled the time when Jeremy and she got stuck in the back seat of her Mitsubishi Eclipse as they pulled up to eat dinner at a restaurant. At the time, Jill was away caring for her ailing mother. Terry and Jeremy consequently stayed at Kelly's house. They decided to go out to eat but only had Kelly's two-seater car with a tiny backseat, if one could call it that. As Kelly got in the backseat, she expected her daughter Patsy to join her while Terry and Jeremy rode up front. Much to her surprise, Jeremy plunged into the backseat with her. However, getting in wasn't the issue. As they pulled into a parking spot, neither Kelly nor Jeremy could budge from the back. They yelled and laughed for a good while then came up with a plan to put the top down so that Terry and Patsy could pull them out. As the wintry air blasted against their faces, Terry and Pasty pulled and yanked to eventually free Kelly and Jeremy from the backseat, while onlookers stared in amusement.

Kelly then turned her thoughts to the fact that Jeremy had revered soldiering his entire life. She recalled the time when he finally became a soldier and a good one. For some reason, she didn't worry about him much during his first combat tour. Perhaps intuition told her that he would return safely, which he did. Jeremy had a purple bandana that he cherished. He gave it to Kelly for safe keeping while deployed overseas. Upon his return, she presented it back to him having kept it safe. She felt as if this ritual showed how Jeremy entrusted her with a piece of his heart during trying times in his life, a commission she gladly embraced. As a result, Jeremy's second tour troubled her deeply. Despite her anguish, Jeremy assured her that everything would be fine and then gave her one of the biggest hugs that she ever received. On the verge of going to combat a second time, he showed more concern for her peace of mind than his own. Jeremy returned safely from his second deployment having had a finger reattached.

Subsequently, it seemed only a short period of time when his third combat tour rolled around. This time, everyone had instinctive angst, even Jeremy himself. Kelly had one of Granddad Smith's old Bibles sitting in her house, which many people had used over the years. Those who studied it wrote sayings and cross-verses in the margins, while highlighted and under-lined scripture accentuated the pages. Jeremy asked if he could read the ven-erated book. With joyful tears rambling down her cheeks, Kelly gave him the cherished Bible. He read it from front to back prior to his deployment, which encouraged both Kelly and Jeremy. Also uplifting, Terry and Jill had a going-away gathering at Lake Barkley on his behalf. Although everyone had a great time, fear subtly gnawed at them in the back of their minds. Then Jeremy, the patriotic gentle giant, gave Kelly and others a reassuring hug, wanting to comfort everyone else despite his unknown fate that awaited him on the other side of the world.

The morning of July 2, 2010, Kelly, along with her daughter, drove to her sister's home to spend a few nights and celebrate the 4th of July, one of her favorite holidays. On the evening of July 3rd, Kelly received a call from Terry and could tell by the sound of his voice that he had bad news about Jeremy. She instantly concluded that the young man met his demise. Before she could speak, Terry stated that Jeremy wasn't dead but got seriously hurt the day before. He had no further details at that moment. Upon receiving the news, Kelly anguished that Jeremy tarried severely wounded in hostile territory. She wanted nothing more than to have him instantly home safe and sound. As helpless panic set in, she began to pray. After what seemed an eternity, the military transported Jeremy to a hospital in Germany. Some-what relieved, Kelly couldn't rest until he finally arrived stateside.

After another eternal wait that gnawed away at Kelly's soul, Jeremy ar-rived at the Walter Reed National Military Medical Center. Engulfed in this troubling ordeal for weeks, Kelly sighed with relief finally experiencing a bit of joy. Shortly thereafter, she received a phone call from him at five in the morning. Oblivious to the early morning hour, she brimmed with excitement. Always more concerned for others than himself, Jeremy said that he would answer any question that she had in order to put her mind at ease. Not concerned with details, Kelly just wanted to listen to his voice. Jeremy assured her that he would be okay. A nurse, Kelly wondered if he truly felt well or if medication gave him a false sense of well-being. Whichever the case, the sound of his strong and confident voice comforted and encouraged her. From then on, Jeremy called her regularly at five in the morning since she usually rose early. Kelly gladly took his calls. Never having texted before, she eagerly learned how so that she and Jeremy could communicate throughout the day.

The time finally arrived when Jeremy could return home to Kentucky. Kelly and Marianne worked feverishly to organize a welcome home family reunion to celebrate the event. They had a banner made that proudly bore several of his pictures, while purple hearts decorated the background. The entire extended Smith family held tremendous regard for the young soldier. When he pulled into the driveway, Kelly could hardly wait to see him. In usual Jeremy fashion, he went around giving everyone a hearty bear hug. When he hugged Kelly, he literally picked her up and set her on the kitchen counter. Thinking back on all this, Kelly ruminated in her soul about how much she missed those wonderful hugs.

This prompted her recollection about the times when Jeremy came just to visit and have movie night, nothing fancy but precious, nonetheless. During these visits, he talked with her about his combat experience, the demons of war, and their effect on his life. The tragedies of combat made him all the more adamant about the importance of family and of preserving the honorable Smith family name. Though a multitude of well-meaning people tried, no one could rid Jeremy of his torments that weighed heavily on his mind. He held Kelly's hand resolutely as he shared his agony with her for hours until he finally fell asleep. She treasured these memories in her heart, the many times when he bared his soul and entrusted her with his pain. During the post-Army years of his life, he battled every hardship head-on, determined to have victory. So many times, Terry, Jill, Leah, and Kelly spent endless hours on the phone discussing Jeremy's plight. Kelly's daughter referred to these conversations as their *conference calls*. During these exchanges, they laughed, cried, and most importantly prayed for Jeremy to regain the simple, happy life that he once had.

These memories poignantly flooded Kelly's mind and heart as she sat ruefully in the room crowded with a myriad of people who came to show their love for Jeremy during this dire time in his life. She ruminated over all the special times that she had with him, the fun, the laughter, the grief, and the tears. Jeremy loved people enormously, bigger than that actually, which was why so many would go to the ends of the earth for him. Jeremy and Kelly often told each other, "I love you to the moon and back." After a while that didn't seem adequate enough. Jeremy started adding planets to the equation. Then Kelly added other solar systems. Eventually, they invoked distant galaxies to express their love for one another.

Despite seeing the world differently at times than Kelly, Jeremy's love for his dear cousin never wavered. His fierce love for family compelled him. This family even included his military brothers and sisters. Jeremy would have done anything to help any of them. He had a heart that big. Kelly remembered a particular time when he borrowed money to help someone in a financial bind. Not explaining to the recipient where the money came from, Jeremy quietly made payments on the loan until repaid in full. Humanity could learn a lesson from Jeremy on how to love a little deeper, sacrifice a little more, and help those in need regardless of one's own personal situation. Reminiscing upon Jeremy, she hoped that she could embrace his attitude in her own life.

Kelly's thoughts then shifted to a lighter venue as she pondered amusing things that Jeremy taught her, such as:

- Jeep makes the prettiest pearl paint in the world.
- Kawasaki green is the best color for frogs.
- You can run from Ms. Piggy, but you can't return to your starting point without paying the price!
- Everyone should write a song in their life.
- Hide a tall man's liquor in the bottom cabinet for he only looks in the top ones.
- Life is better with cereal!
- Make infomercials when shopping.
- Forget lunch and go for the milkshake!

◆◆◆

Heartbroken over Jeremy's disposition, Donna Mink, his aunt, reminisced about the first time that she met him in 2013. Having married into the Smith extended family, her husband Scott and she celebrated Thanksgiving at Terry's and Jill's home that year. When Jeremy walked into the room, Donna marveled at his larger-than-life gentle-giant persona. He took his uncle Scott for a ride in his Corvette. Upon their return, Donna eagerly pleaded for a ride in the muscle car as well. When Jeremy obliged, she resolutely requested that he drive the same way for her as he did for his uncle. As they sped off, she felt completely at ease. Jeremy had a way of making her feel safe even while driving way to fast in a Corvette. Recalling these events brought a smile to her face despite the somberness of the day.

Donna remembered Jeremy's visit a few years later when he spent the weekend with them at their Indiana home. He brought his guitar with him and played it at her brother's party. Everyone loved listening to him strumming the guitar and singing. Donna absolutely loved hearing him perform. He could play just about any song whether serious or humorous. Jeremy played from his heart and didn't keep proper time, so trained musicians found it difficult to keep pace with him. He touched so many people that night with his anointed talents that they still asked about him today. With a broken spirit, Donna informed them that PTSD got the better of him. Her answer generated shock and dismay among her friends and relatives, because Jeremy had touched their souls so deeply that weekend.

Donna then remembered one of the most profound moments that Jeremy and she shared. When Great Aunt Margie passed away, Scott was one of the pallbearers at her funeral. As the pallbearers prepared to carry the casket to the hearse, Donna stepped outside to wait with the rest of the family. Greif stricken, she desperately tried to hold back her tears. Jeremy walked up and asked her a question. Looking up at him with forlorn eyes, she struggled to speak but to no avail. She simply held up a finger to signal a request for a moment to compose herself before responding. He quickly discerned the anguish and put his arm around her confirming that everything would be okay. His timely comfort and genuine concern forged an unbreakable bond between Jeremy and his despondent aunt. She never forgot that moment, that day, or how the soft-hearted gentle giant loved his family.

Donna recalled the last time that she spoke to Jeremy during the month of July 2018. She could tell that he battled a demon from which he just couldn't get away. She couldn't determine exactly what issue so tormented him and desperately hoped that he would successfully work through it. Thinking of his current condition, she teared up and began to cry. Only this time, no gentle giant stood beside her to offer comfort. Beneath her quiet sobs, Donna woefully wished that the world had more Jeremys in it.

♦♦♦

With a profoundly broken heart, Jeremy's uncle, Scott Mink, grimaced at his nephew's current situation. Having grown up in different states, they gathered together as family during major holidays such as Thanksgiving and Christmas. Over the years they also kept in touch mostly by phone. Scott reminisced about how his outgoing nephew loved to play the guitar and make up songs along the way. A real jokester, Jeremy composed some very humorous ballads. Jeremy never seemed to have a bad day except when someone wanted to take Leah out on a date. Scott got to know Jeremy well because his nephew, as a teenager, often stayed with him over the summer. In those years, Scott had a racing team. Jeremy enjoyed going with them to the track. Not only did this give them an avenue to bond as good friends, but it also instilled a fervor within Jeremy for hot rods and fast trucks. They often played racing video games during which Jeremy competed furiously.

Scott thought about how Jeremy wanted to join the military after 9/11. He finally did so in 2003 but had to lose a lot of weight in a certain amount of time. Because of that, Jeremy dieted and worked out feverishly during a two-month visit with his uncle. Determined to prove to the recruiters his worthiness to serve in the Army and fight in combat, he lost what seemed like a hundred pounds in those two months. He showed great discipline, which deeply inspired his uncle. Having met the military height/weight requirements, Jeremy went on active duty and became a great warrior known as *Big Country*. When he came home from his first and second combat deployments, he still seemed like Jeremy as far as Scott could tell. However, during the third deployment when his transport vehicle got blown up, everything changed in an instant. The Jeremy that Scott knew and loved never returned home from Afghanistan. The wounded body of his beloved nephew came home, but his mind, heart, and soul never did. They had changed forever as depression ate away at the once great warrior. Scott grieved deeply over the plight of his nephew. Life and the family would never be the same.

♦♦♦

Gazing about the solemn room, Jill's sister, Sharri Condon, recalled how Jeremy emerged as the first and the biggest in many ways in the family. He hailed as Jill's first born, the first great-grandson for Granny, the first grandson for her mom, and her first nephew. At the tender age of twenty, Sharri had no children of her own and eagerly looked forward to becoming an aunt. Then he arrived. Jeremy Doyle Smith came into the world big, weighing over ten pounds. He then embarked on living a big life with his big heart, big smile, big laugh, and especially big hugs. Whenever Jeremy hugged her, he imparted genuine love to her, which made her feel special. It came as no surprise to her that his comrades-in-arms felt sincere love from him and affectionately called him *Big Country*. His life had a big impact on everyone he knew.

Sharri reminisced about Jeremy's early childhood years. She got to spend most of her time with him then before he moved from Indianapolis to Franklin. She thought how he never wanted to disappoint anyone, always a good little boy and very polite. She remembered most his desire to serve in the Army like his daddy. He almost always dressed in camo, enlisting his younger sister Leah as often as he could. Sharri babysat for Jill and Terry often, sometimes picking the children up from daycare on Friday and staying with them until Sunday. Whenever she babysat, pizza, movies, and cookies abounded. At some point, Jeremy and Leah gave her the name *Aunt Cookie*.

Looking at her nephew lying so still and quiet, she remembered, out of the blue, how he also loved the ninja turtles. Then she recalled a weekend when she drove Jeremy to Granny's house in Kentucky. Sitting up front with her like a big boy, a five-year-old Jeremy inquired, "So what kind of juice you put in this crate?" He then proceeded to tell her a big story. Sharri couldn't recall the details but remembered that it seemed a little far-fetched. So, she gave him a doubtful look and asked, "Is that really true, Jeremy?"

With a really big laugh, he said, "No Aunt Cookie, I was just pulling your chain." His big personality, his big story telling, his big laugh, and his big smile blessed everyone. After Terry and Jill moved to Kentucky, Sharri didn't see Jeremy much except for an occasional weekend or holiday visit. Regardless, every one of his cousins adored him. He would play with them and let them torture him, all with a big smile on his face.

Sharri's mind then fast forwarded to sometime after Jeremy graduated from high school. She remembered him working so hard to join the Army. When he came back from basic training, she hardly recognized him. His eyes had changed, no longer having the innocent look they once had. Tragically, with each tour of duty, his eyes became more and more distant, as though he couldn't look at you, as if he dwelled somewhere else. He would still entertain everyone with big stories, big smiles, and big laughs. However, he drank too much to hide the pain that no one else could possibly understand. When he got injured, he could no longer continue with what he knew best—soldiering. Sharri thought about how Jeremy struggled relentlessly to come back to them, fighting to find peace in this world.

Finally, Sharri reminisced about the joint birthday party that she had with Leah that June. Sharri's birth date was three days after Leah's. A warm delight filled Sharri's heart as she remembered Jeremy driving to Bowling Green to buy her a special cake, a cookie cake, for his Aunt Cookie. She knew undoubtedly that he loved her so very much. Anyone who knew

Jeremy would feel the same way. He simply loved family and friends deeply with that great big heart of his.

♦ ♦ ♦

Ellen Condon quietly looked around the room at all the unfamiliar faces that came to her cousin Jeremy's side in his time of despair. Although she didn't know them, she was confident that they knew and loved her cousin profoundly. She wondered how Jeremy had touched their lives. For her, he inspired her most with music. Most of her passion for music came from moments as a child with Jeremy. When he sang and played the guitar, he had a magical power about him. Ellen could see that he didn't just play music, rather he poured out his soul. Playing various types of guitars became a huge part of his identity. Jeremy also displayed much confidence through his deep, rich voice. He clung to these talents as therapy so many times in his life, not only for himself but for others as well. While home from war during family holiday gatherings, he mended and bonded everyone together with songs from the past and present.

Whenever Ellen played guitar, she felt as if Jeremy played alongside her. Terry and Jill gave her one of Jeremy's old guitars. It was even signed by the members of his former band. The words written on the guitar spoke loudly about the love that Jeremy could put in the heart of anyone anywhere. With this talent, no walls could keep him from reaching a person that he wanted to touch. At first, she hesitated to play that sacred instrument. When she finally did, a myriad of profound thoughts and senses came to her as she reverently played. She strummed the same strings that he did in situations much worse than any place of despair in which she ever found herself. She remembered the quiet shaking of the sand inside as the instrument vibrated. She realized that this sand came from one of the deserts in which he fought and bled. She pondered the times when her cousin must have found solace for his soul in hostile surroundings by playing this guitar. In those moments, in some way, the hollow body of the instrument, along with its beautiful sounds, offered salvation to him somewhere in a war-torn land. Playing Jeremy's guitar now gave her that same salvation.

Ellen reflected upon the many negative effects that protecting our country had on Jeremy. He carried a heavy load that would crush any normal person. However, to her, this in itself displayed Jeremy's great beauty. Stronger than most, he never let these burdens diminish his love for others. He never lost his empathy for those who showed an ounce of good. Without regret, he stood for righteousness and fought evil. Jeremy greatly influenced the person who Ellen became. He taught her to love music and use it to spread love. She pondered how Jeremy was real, good, loyal, honest, and all the things that made the world better. This inspired her to be like him. This craving made him part of her soul. It gave her a profound desire to improve for the better, to love more deeply, to dive passionately into everything she did, and to have an intense determination to make a positive difference. Ellen decided in her heart to chase this craving until she caught it. She knew that within her soul Jeremy would smile and belly laugh the whole time. And once she captured this craving, a big Jeremy bear hug awaited her in that moment.

♦ ♦ ♦

Mike Smith sat in the crowded room staring at his cousin, the deportment of both men silent, expressionless. Jeremy seemed more like a brother to Mike than a cousin, always his best friend, the best man at his wedding, and quick to tell anyone how much he looked up to Mike, ten years his senior. On the contrary though, Jeremy had a more profound impact on Mike's life. They spent most of their childhood summers together running around the woods and creeks of west Kentucky. At that time, Jeremy, in the prime of his childhood, idolized Mike in all his 1990s glory, complete with a mullet haircut, fast car, electric guitar, and few cares in the world. During these summer escapades, Mike taught Jeremy a little about playing the guitar. Later in life, however, Jeremy taught Mike more about music and guitar than Mike ever taught him.

Both cousins shared the desire to serve their country in the Army. They spent untold hours fighting battles and running crucial missions on the farm and in the nearby woods. Mike smiled slightly as he remembered how he would aggravate Jeremy during these excursions. Mike found great humor in dampening Jeremy's army fantasies by not playing up to the level of grandeur that Jeremy expected, even demanded. When Jeremy chose his moniker, usually *General Ironsides* or something cool like that, Mike insisted on being *Private Gumdrop* or something far less glorious. Every time, consternation engulfed Jeremy for this hailed as serious business for the seven-year-old. Eventually, the lad relented and soon the command of *Private Gumdrop, charge!* rang throughout the hills of the small farm for a good part of the day. Mike considered these some of the best times of their lives.

Regrettably, Mike suffered from a hereditary blood condition called Thalassemia, which kept him from entering military service. Consequently, while Mike became the first Smith male never to serve the country in the military, Jeremy went on to become one of the most decorated servicemen in the family. He took great pride in his younger cousin. During his college days and later during Jeremy's years in high school, the two cousins struggled for time to spend together. Regardless, their bond never weakened. Years later when Jeremy returned from his first deployment, they began to spend more time together, as their bachelor lives matched up perfectly. Between deployments, Mike fell in with Jeremy and his military buddies every chance he got—meeting girls, driving fast, playing guitars, shooting, shooting, and doing more shooting.

Mike recalled how, during this period, Jeremy humbly strove to exalt everyone else around him rather than himself. He constantly introduced Mike to his Army friends, decorated military combat veterans, the best of the best, as the guy who taught him everything he knew. Jeremy boasted how those days playing army in the woods with Mike taught him so many things which later saved his life in combat. Appreciative of the flattery, Mike felt confident that his cousin's military training had more to do with that than he did. Regardless, Jeremy never let Mike look down on himself. Mike marveled at his cousin's big, loud, yet humble demeanor, an unusual combination. Jeremy loomed as the biggest and the loudest guy in the room on behalf of everyone else first and himself last.

In those days, Mike and Jeremy engaged in many comedic exploits, the most constant and funniest were voice impressions, something Mike started in their younger days that Jeremy quickly mastered. Innumerable times, the voice of Arnold Schwarzenegger or the Karl Childers character from the movie *Sling Blade* showed up at Sonic to order biscuits and mustard. As their favorite routine, they spoke a mishmash of British and Australian accents. In so doing, they quickly discovered that this attracted the young ladies, who didn't seem to care if the accents switched between the two dialects in the same discourse. Acting like they had just gotten to America, Mike and Jeremy struck up a conversation over the speaker, inquiring about everything, even asking for a description of a cheeseburger. Without fail, a starry-eyed girl, smiling from ear to ear, came out with their food, eager to continue the conversation with the *British boys*. The charade began to crack when the young lady got her first look at Mike and Jeremy. It completely fell apart when they shifted into the most obnoxious redneck impersonations the two men could muster, hilarious for them and momentarily heartbreaking for the young lady, who usually took it in good spirits.

A somber mood overtook Mike as he reminisced about the time that Jeremy got seriously wounded. A bittersweet scenario prevailed as he felt immense pride toward his younger cousin, who fought valiantly in combat, mixed with extreme broken heartedness. The severe wound drastically altered Jeremy's future military service, jeopardizing his lifelong dream of an Army career. Having recently bought a house only a few miles from

Jeremy's, Mike spent even more time with his injured cousin. Music became the primary therapy. Mike wondered how they didn't completely wear out those guitars. With heaviness in his heart, Mike pondered the regret he felt for lacking the ability to help his cousin deal with what he now referred to as Jeremy's demons. Jeremy refused to show weakness making it difficult for anyone to enter his inner chamber of pain. In addition, Mike couldn't relate to what his cousin felt because he never experienced combat. He had a few mildly harrowing experiences during his time as a volunteer firefighter but nothing that remotely compared to what Jeremy encountered. Despite the darkness, Jeremy always encouraged Mike and wanted the best for him.

Shortly before Jeremy's mishap that brought all these people together, Mike visited him out of happenstance. On Mike's birthday, he and his son went fishing. An unknown force drew them to a fishing spot near Terry's and Jill's house. On the way home, they found themselves on the quiet country road that Jeremy now called home and stopped in for a visit. Mike rejoiced at the thought that Jeremy recently quit drinking, played in the worship group at church, and strove to get his life back to normal, finally turning the corner. Jeremy met them in the driveway where they stood and talked a while. Soaking wet from wading in a river and eager to get home, Mike and his son politely lingered so Jeremy could show them some trigger-work he had done on a pistol and give Mike's son a box of ammo. Something told Mike not to leave right away but to savor the moment. When they finally left, an unseen influence compelled Mike to stop, get out of the vehicle, and give his cousin a hearty hug. Mike asked him if he was okay. Jeremy smiled and replied, "Never better,"—Mike's last memory of his beloved cousin.

♦♦♦

Chris Wood gazed upon the gentle giant across the room as tears welled up in her eyes. She and her husband Jeff met Jill and Terry approximately twenty-four years ago when the Smith family moved to Franklin, Kentucky. The day that they met, they all became more like family than friends. Chris and Jeff immediately fell in love with Terry, Jill, and their children. The Woods had two boys of their own named Jeffery and Brandon, both about Leah's age. Jeremy adopted the two young lads, who looked up to him as a big brother. Whenever visiting, he gave them his undivided attention, entertaining them usually with army play. Chris had never before seen that level of genuine concern and compassion in such a young boy. As usual, Jeremy impressed them in a big way. He always greeted them politely at the door, the onset of each visit containing a huge Jeremy-hug for each of her boys, then off to playland while the grownups visited. Afterward, Jeffery and Brandon could hardly wait for the next visit.

Chris believed that Jeremy had a special affinity for Brandon because of his tiny stature. Jeremy continually carried the little tyke on his hip, covering him under guardian wing. Brandon, in turn, discerned Jeremy's genuine love and affectionately clung to him as if superglued to the gentle giant. He frequently ran his tiny hand through Jeremy's fiery hair as a show of perfect brotherly love. Jeremy always had an army game to play. He treasured his G.I. Joes yet never hesitated to allow Jeffery and Brandon to play with these prized possessions of his. He also played video games with them. He often lay on the floor and let Brandon and Jeffery just lay all over him as a big pillow. They loved to wrestle as boys do. However, Jeremy never let them get hurt during the tussles, always the mindful guardian. When Jeremy babysat her boys, Chris felt confident that she left them in good hands. Jeremy never disappointed her.

The boys stayed in contact throughout the years. Unbeknownst to Chris and Jeff at the time, a bully shoved and pushed Brandon around while in high school. As soon as Jeremy found out, he put an immediate stop to it. When Chris heard about this years later, she recalled Jill saying how Jeremy always took up for bullied kids, protecting those who couldn't defend themselves. She then remembered that Jeremy was part of her boys' youth group in their church. They always viewed him as a big loving giant. His heart was always toward the benefit of others, a good protector and mentor for the younger boys.

Chris reflected upon the time when Jeff and she, along with his parents visiting from Missouri, ate at a restaurant. Jeremy, a graduate from high school at this juncture, spotted them and politely stopped at their table to say hello. He made a point to ask Jeff's parents how they were, even though he didn't know them. Upon introductions, Jeremy shook Jeff's dad's hand, making a big impression upon the elder man. When Jeremy left, Jeff's dad, a decent sized man, marveled at the young man's handshake and cordiality. He commented that Jeremy's handshake was the most genuine he had ever felt, firm yet gentle despite Jeremy's size and strength. This gentle giant's massive hand conveyed nothing but love for humanity.

Chris then remembered attending Leah's twenty-fifth birthday party, where Jeremy gave rides in his Corvette over the back roads of the county. She gasped with delight when he hit those high speeds yet didn't feel afraid. She thoroughly trusted him and no other with her life in that circumstance. Wanting to go for another thrilling spin, she declined because Jeremy refused to accept any gas money from anyone.

Chris thought about how Jeremy's humor equaled his kindness, love, and consideration. At gatherings, he made everyone laugh without fail regardless of the atmosphere. He had an innate ability to grab everybody's attention and draw them into the antics using satire and gestures. He made sure that he left out no one. His goal was not to garnish attention for himself but to make sure that everyone felt joy, inclusion, love, and worth. A great man of character, he deeply impacted all their lives and inspired her boys to become good men.

◆◆◆

Betty Raines thought back to August 1997 when she first noticed the blazon red hair of an eighth-grade student attending Franklin-Simpson Middle School. She always loved red hair especially since it ran in her family; her oldest son had such colored hair. She noticed over the years that some students didn't like their red hair, so she made it a point to let them know what a beautiful color it was for hair. Her first words spoken to Jeremy Smith conveyed how much she loved his. Betty remembered what a good student Jeremy was in her U.S. History class. Self-motivated, eager to learn, and never disruptive, he always did his best in class and showed perfect politeness as a young gentleman who never failed to say *yes, ma'am* or *no, ma'am* when addressing Mrs. Raines. Besides the red hair, Betty noticed that Jeremy always had a smile on his face and a twinkle in his eyes, never acting out for attention as did other students. Getting along well with others, he worked hard, studied hard, and had a great attitude. He played football and participated in speech competitions all the while maintaining good grades. He left a lasting impression on her heart.

As the years passed, Jeremy graduated from high school and Betty retired from teaching. One morning, she saw Jill Smith, who asked her to pray for Jeremy while in the military serving in the Middle East. Betty gladly agreed and diligently did so. A couple of years later, Betty became friends with Jill on Facebook where she read the *Stars and Stripes* article about Jeremy's heroic deeds in Afghanistan. From this article, she discovered that Jeremy served in the 101st Airborne, the same division in which her brother served in Vietnam from 1965 to 1966. They both came home from war with seen and unseen wounds. PTSD had a traumatic impact on Jeremy's life, as it did on her brother's. She didn't get to see Jeremy after he came home from war but did connect with him on Facebook. She sent him birthday wishes and thanked him for his service to the country, which he humbly received, always the gentle giant.

Jeremy never made a big deal out of his military service. Proud to serve his country, he didn't do it to draw notice to himself, even though he received two purple hearts, three army achievement medals, three army commendation medals (one for valor), and a bronze star. Through Facebook, Betty also discovered that Jeremy loved to sing and play guitar. She felt that his life story would have been perfect for Paul Harvey's *The Rest of the Story*. When she taught Jeremy in middle school, she only knew him daily for about a year, not realizing the hero that he would become. Now, she knew that he carried the scars of combat, like her brother, every day in his mind, heart, and soul. Betty never revealed to Jeremy that her brother suffered severely from PTSD. She didn't tell him about the many hours in which they sat, talked, and cried about his experiences in the Vietnam War. Because she loved her brother dearly, his torment became hers. Little did she know while teaching the polite, red-haired boy in middle school, how, later in life, they would both partake much in the sufferings required by freedom and liberty.

Betty recently reminisced through the yearbook when Jeremy attended eighth grade. The theme that year was "Leaving Our Mark." How profound that Jeremy fulfilled this calling, for he truly left his mark on the lives of so many people. The caption at the top of the page displaying his picture proclaimed, "Good Impressions." This spoke volumes of Jeremy too. During the course of her teaching career, Betty taught over three thousand students. Jeremy Smith always stood out in her memory, leaving his mark and making a good impression on her heart. He did the same with the men and women with whom he served in the Army. History books recorded the dates, places, and major military leaders of battles and wars. They seldom chronicled the actions of so many anonymous soldiers who made the ultimate sacrifice during the ravages of combat or whose lives forever changed protecting our freedom and liberty. Betty sorely wished that more books told the stories of these unsung heroes.

◆ ◆ ◆

Ryan Masching thought back to his sophomore year in high school. He had just moved to Franklin, Kentucky and knew no one. Riding the bus to school, he heard a couple of boys laughing, telling jokes, and having a good time at the back of the bus. Noticing Ryan as the new kid, Jeremy called out for him to sit back there with them, which he did. The first to befriend Ryan, Jeremy and he became good friends soon after. A year behind Jeremy, Ryan recalled that his friend worked at Sonic, and the two of them hung out as time allowed. In 2001, Jeremy graduated from high school and signed Ryan's yearbook as follows, "Ryan, stay cool man, have fun next year. Destroy the penguin invasion. Remember Ryan, 185 days of school and you'll be signing your friend's yearbook. Stay cool man. Keep in touch. May the desires of your heart be the realities of your hand." The penguin invasion referenced a skit from the show *Monty Python's Flying Circus*. That particular skit made Jeremy laugh uncontrollably and became a recurring line of jest between the two of them for years to come. When one of them needed a pick-me-up, the other declared in an English accent, "There's a penguin on the tele." Jeremy became masterful at using that line to lighten a sullen mood.

During Ryan's senior year in high school, he decided to join the Marine Corps. Knowing Jeremy's affinity for military service, he talked Jeremy into joining the Corps as well and took him to his recruiter. Unfortunately, Jeremy didn't meet the height/weight standards. This became a great loss for the Marine Corps, as Jeremy later joined the Army and proved himself an outstanding soldier. He would have emerged as one hell of a Marine. Jeremy helped Ryan prepare for boot camp through vigorous workouts and yelling different lines from the movie *Full Metal Jacket* at one another, defying the other not to laugh while standing at attention. Smiling slightly, Ryan conceded that these deportment drills didn't prepare him much for military training but made for some unforgettable memories with one of the best people he had ever known.

The rivalry between the Army and Marines compelled the two friends to poke fun at one another, each man declaring himself tougher than the other. In all seriousness, Ryan marveled at the valiant warrior that Jeremy became, as well as his stories of training, different duty stations, friends made and lost along the way, and times in battle. In his heart, Ryan felt profoundly fortunate to have met Jeremy Smith.

♦♦♦

Michael Hines pondered the days when he worked at Sonic as a teenager in high school. His first job, he remembered meeting another wide-eyed new employee named Jeremy Smith. They became good friends and hung out together frequently. Michael could always rely on him to help with his problems, be it with girls or a fight he had with his dad. Jeremy became like a brother to him. When Michael first moved out on his own, Jeremy gladly helped with the heavy lifting. Michael could count on him for anything. In fact, Jeremy not only helped his friends, but he also never hesitated to help a stranger either.

Michael recalled the time when they went to Walmart late one night after work. A slight smile adorned Michael's face as he concluded to himself that a person definitely knew that he lived in a small town if he hung out at Walmart after work. Standing in line at the checkout then came to mind. A couple with a small child checked out in front of them, attempting to buy groceries and toiletries. Unfortunately, they didn't have enough money to purchase both and elected to forgo the toiletries. Jeremy stepped up and told the cashier that he would pay for those items. The couple stood there speechless as he placed the bag into their buggy. They thanked him repeatedly. The cashier had a pin on her collar given to her by Walmart for helping others. She took it off and put it on Jeremy's shirt, saying that he deserved it more than she.

To Michael, Jeremy loomed as one in a million. He hated to see him join the Army and go away but knew it was his lifelong dream. They always told each other to never change and did their best to keep in touch over the years. Michael pursed his lips as he wished that he did a better job of that especially over the past few years. From the last few times that he talked to Jeremy, Michael took joy in knowing that, despite all he went through, Jeremy's big heart for people never changed. He always wanted to help others and take the weight off their shoulders by gladly bearing the burden himself.

$$\blacklozenge\ \blacklozenge\ \blacklozenge$$

Megan Smith remembered the October day in 2017 when she first met Jeremy Smith, whom she considered a truly amazing man. Although they had the same last name, they weren't related. Shortly after Jeremy moved back to Franklin, Kentucky, he came into the office where Megan worked. She, subsequently, assisted him with his issue. Unfortunately, they had to resolve some glitches relating to his matter. Megan spent as much time as needed to ensure that this got done properly. While working out the details, she had the chance to talk with him a bit. In so doing, she learned that they had a mutual acquaintance. Megan went to school with Leah, Jeremy's sister. Megan remembered how Leah talked about her big brother all the time, in whom she took so much pride. Now, Megan experienced for herself how easy and delightful it was to speak with him.

The next day, Jeremy returned to that office, spoke with the supervisor, and extolled great compliments on Megan for her great attitude and thorough work. Such laudatory feedback didn't happen often. Jeremy had no obligation to do this, which gave her the first glimpse of his big-heartedness. During the conversation with the supervisor, Megan also found out that he served in the Army. Megan's boss then sincerely thanked him for his service to the country. He immediately replied, "It was my honor to serve ma'am, and I would go back tomorrow if they would let me." His sincere servant's mindset made a profound impression on Megan.

After his conversation with her supervisor, Megan reached out to him and thanked him for the kind words. He responded, "Everybody wants to fuss and complain when people do a bad job, but they hardly ever speak up when somebody goes out of their way to do something good."

The two of them really hit it off after that, continuing to see each other often. Despite his gruff appearance, Jeremy behaved without fail as a perfect gentleman to Megan—the kind who walked up to the front door to pick a young lady up, the kind who opened and shut the car door for her, the one who walked on the outside of the sidewalk, the one who just made a young lady feel perfectly safe in his presence. They stayed up late so many nights talking for hours. He opened his soul to her, making her feel safe to do the same. She found him to be one of the most honest people that she ever met, never sugarcoating anything. If he said something edifying or critical, he meant it genuinely. Jeremy faced so much trauma both while in the military and afterward. He dealt with things that Megan couldn't fathom or help resolve—deep, dark specters that affected him each and every day.

Megan knew without a doubt that Jeremy cherished his time in the military, the greatest highlight of his life. He often declared that he flourished and lived at his best during that time, having a great sense of purpose. Impeccable at what he did, he embodied unmatched loyalty to his country and to his brothers-in-arms. Jeremy always referred to those with whom he served as his brothers. Megan could tell that he loved them just as if they had been born natural brothers, caring for and trusting them like no other. The expression on his face lit up with joy and pride whenever he talked about one of them, extolling their bravery and honor. Each time Megan complimented Jeremy on his service, he immediately gave the glory to his brothers, seeing the best in each and every one of them. He worried about their problems more than he did his own. Without hesitation, he took their burdens upon his own shoulders. He often spoke to Megan of their struggles and their triumphs. At a moment's notice, he availed himself to do whatever he could to help a struggling brother.

Ominous things that Jeremy experienced overseas haunted him daily. He shared with Megan some of the trauma that he faced while serving. She knew in her heart that he concealed far darker tragedies of which he simply couldn't talk. Sometimes this menacing darkness pulled him down for days at a time. Jeremy referred to it as drowning. Megan recalled one conversation that they had on the anniversary date of the demise of two fallen brothers. She tried desperately to help him escape the dark place in which he frantically drowned. Despite her best effort, nothing she said helped because she didn't relate to that situation through her own personal experiences in life. She suggested that he talk to one of his brothers about it, someone who could understand and relate to the torment with which Jeremy dealt. Much to Megan's chagrin, he flatly refused to heap one bit of his burdensome anguish upon any of his brothers. He simply wouldn't entertain the notion of dragging his brothers down into the darkness with him by taking them back to those dreadful days of combat in their minds. He never wanted to do anything that might cause pain to the people he loved.

Jeremy always wanted to be the strong one, the one on whom everyone else could count. Many of his brothers contacted him during their struggles. He consoled and encouraged every one of them without hesitation. He gladly became an outlet for their grief even though he denied himself that same opportunity. He hated going to group meetings but would do so if it helped one of his brothers. He subjected himself to reliving the worst days of his life if one of his brothers wanted to talk about it. However, like a selfless big brother, he never asked for that same consideration in return. To simply call Jeremy a good man understated the superb quality of this gentle giant. He confined a multitude of demons within his soul to shield his comrades from grief, yet it couldn't tarnish his heart of gold. To the people he loved, he proved a fierce protector, a trusted confidant, and a man on which one could count. He always found a way to make people laugh, making jokes out of the most random things, his infectious laugh lighting up the whole room. An amazing storyteller, he just had a way with words, brilliantly expressing himself in song, music, or just talking to someone. Megan often marveled at his larger-than-life persona. Unlike anyone she had ever met, Jeremy changed her life forever.

◆◆◆

Mike Keel grew up in Hopkinsville, Kentucky. Earning a living in the construction industry, he worked his way up to executive management over the years. Interacting with several military veterans who now worked in construction gave Mike an idea of what they went through in combat and life thereafter. He saw firsthand how combat veterans dealt with PTSD, TBI, and the struggle to get adequate care. The military and VA care systems seemed to be a pill factory of zombie drugs for treatment. Constantly prescribing such drugs didn't cure anyone and often caused more problems than it solved. Witnessing all this instilled within Mike a great appreciation and compassion for combat veterans. So much so that he began to participate in veterans' support groups on Facebook. Consequently, he struck up a friendship with a certain veteran who stood out among the rest. They called him Big Country, and the two of them became good friends even though they would never meet in person.

The news of Jeremy's current condition devastated Mike. He recalled how they used to text each other often and the many telephone conversations they had. Over time, Mike learned of Jeremy's struggle with PTSD, as well as with a leg wound that wouldn't fully heal. Jeremy dealt with pain and discomfort every day and couldn't get the proper attention that he needed from the VA medical services. Mike took a great interest in Jeremy's health and welfare. As a result, he also developed friendships with Jeremy's parents, Terry and Jill. Mike offered his support to many veterans who consequently called him at all hours of the night needing encouragement. Mike gladly obliged. Jeremy knew that he could call Mike anytime about anything. Both Kentucky boys, Jeremy found Mike easy to talk to because he displayed great understanding and sympathy. Often, hurting veterans simply needed a caring and compassionate ear to listen to them.

Shortly after connecting with Jeremy, Mike discerned that Big Country was a big ol' boy with an even bigger heart. Jeremy constantly expressed grief to Mike that his issues caused despair for his family and friends, something Jeremy never wanted. This consumed Jeremy to the point that he focused more on shielding others from his problems and demons than on dealing directly with these issues to heal himself. Mike always felt that Jeremy needed to concentrate on resolving his personal problems first. However, Jeremy always put others ahead of himself, especially his parents and sister. Despite his many struggles, Jeremy cared more about their impact on others than on himself. Jeremy's love for family and selflessness toward others impressed Mike. Without causing others to suffer, Jeremy just wanted to get healed on the inside, get his leg fixed, become good ol' Big Country again, and continue on with his life as before. Knowing of Jeremy's great love for others, Mike asked him on one occasion to reach out to another combat veteran who struggled greatly and tried to commit suicide. Jeremy did so without hesitation and helped him cope with his personal demons. He understood personally what combat veterans experienced and what they currently went through emotionally.

Jeremy lamented to Mike that he drank too much alcohol to cope with the emotional and physical pain. Mike told him not to condemn himself over it because he had more stressors in his life than the typical person. Jeremy confided with Mike that seeing his brothers-in-arms hurt or killed in battle cut deeply into his soul and left lasting torments on his psyche. The civilian collateral damage that he saw during armed conflict also bothered him greatly. He wished that only the combatants would get hurt in battle and war, sparing the civilian populous, especially the children. Witnessing the ravages of war upon civilians grieved him deeply. His compassionate heart for humanity ironically imposed this bane upon his soul.

7

The Brotherhood

SITTING ON THE FRONT porch gazing over his farm, SSG Eric Pollack got a call from an army buddy who told him that Big Country had a terrible mishap. Eric sat there in disbelief and pondered the injustice of it all. One of the finest people ever, Jeremy had a great impact on Eric's life. His influence yielded the best parts of Eric's soul. He left for Franklin, Kentucky a few days later to show his support for Big Country and his family. Reuniting with all the brothers-in-arms that assembled there encouraged Eric. Each one of them brought out the best of the others. They all shined brightest when together as a whole. Seeing Jeremy there in that horrible condition resulted in the saddest day of Eric's life. However, it brought him and many of his brothers back together who hadn't seen each other for years.

Eric began to ponder his life. He grew up in Fort Lauderdale, Florida. Working as a cook in a steakhouse, he decided to join the Army, something he wanted to do for a while to provide a better life for his wife and children. His wife rejoiced upon hearing the news, looking forward to a better quality of life with a steady paycheck and benefits. Eric's father served in the Military Police in Vietnam, and both grandfathers served in World War II, one in the Army and one in the Navy. Eric left for basic training on April 10, 2000, at the age of twenty-one. He served as a combat engineer. His first assignment occurred at Fort Carson, Colorado. After that, he spent the rest of his time at Fort Wainwright, Alaska. He deployed to Iraq with the 562nd Engineer Company in 2005 and later with the 73rd Engineers in 2008.

Eric thought back to when he first met Jeremy in the 562nd as it transitioned from a light to a stryker unit in 2003 and 2004. As a result, the company received an influx of new soldiers which included Big Country as a brand new private. When Eric went to the welcome center to pick up

a batch of newbies, he noticed this mountain of a man. New privates usually came with problems and issues, but Jeremy proved himself intelligent,
down to earth, bighearted, respectful, and professional. Eric presumed that
this hulking young man would be cocky with attitude problems. However,
Jeremy's professional mindset positively influenced the other soldiers who
looked to him as a natural leader. Big Country's persona and character simply drew them to him.

Jeremy and Eric served in the same platoon while on deployment. No
matter what the circumstance, Big Country always showed a positive outlook
on things. If anything bothered him, he held it in and hid it from others. During downtime, they sat around, drank "near" beer, and talked about home,
as well as what they wanted to do with the rest of their lives. They developed
such a close brotherhood that any of them could show up at Eric's home now,
kick in the door, sit down to a beer, and chat about old times. As a close-knit
group, they talked, cared for, and carried each other when down.

During the 2005 deployment, SSG Pollack worked in the tactical operations center (TOC) before becoming a squad leader, replacing a SGT who
got severely injured when his Stryker vehicle got blown off a bridge. During
this deployment, his unit received accolades for the myriad of IEDs that they
discovered and neutralized. However, Eric encountered forty-plus IEDs that
exploded nearby, injuring his brain, shoulder, and back. The shock waves of
the concussion blast caused TBI. Even though this deployment scarred him
for life, it also blessed him. One day while patrolling in Anbar Province, they
came upon a farm that significantly impacted Eric. In the middle of hell and
destruction everywhere, this farm grew life from the earth. This experience
inspired him to become a farmer after his military career.

SSG Pollack recalled a patrol when the lead Stryker vehicle hit an IED
which blew out every tire and created a crater that engulfed the vehicle. Miraculously, all the soldiers riding within survived that deafening blast. When
the smoke cleared, everyone checked themselves for wounds. Fortunately,
only their vehicles suffered damage. Most of the enemy action consisted of
an IED detonation, ensuing small arms fire, and then enemy displacement.
Often times, U.S. soldiers found it difficult to identify where the hostile fire
came from because the enemy combatants dressed just like the local populous. If the engineers located the enemy, they laid down suppressive fire and
called in the infantry to neutralize the threat, so they could leave the scene
and continue on with their mission of clearing the routes of IEDs. If the
engineers couldn't check the segment of a route within a designated window
of time, it was no longer considered safe for other military traffic.

Eric then remembered an instance when he and his squad had a bad
day, with morale and attitudes extremely low prior to embarking on their

mission. Discerning this, Big Country went to Eric and asked, "Hey, are you doing okay, SGT?"

Eric replied, "No I need a big pick-me-up."

Jeremy then physically picked up the five-foot-ten, two-hundred-pound SGT with all his gear on as if a bag of feathers and carried him around the motor pool in front of the entire squad. Setting Eric back down, Jeremy asked, "Is that a big enough pick-me-up, SGT?"

The entire squad erupted in laughter, exactly what the unit needed at that moment. At other times when morale faltered, Jeremy picked up his guitar and played, drawing in those around him. This helped them deal with the loneliness of missing home and loved ones. Eric marveled at Big Country's natural ability as an entertainer.

SSG Pollack reminisced about a specific mission where Jeremy's expertise in mathematics, calculations, and explosives came in handy. They had to demolish a police station in Rawa, Iraq, where a rogue police officer rammed a car bomb into the side of the building rendering it unstable. The authorities asked the U.S. forces to raze the structure so they could build a park in which the children could play. The engineers had to use extreme caution and a small amount of explosives because a mosque sat across the street. They couldn't allow for any collateral damage to other buildings. As they planned out the location and amount of explosives, Jeremy stated off the top of his head to place them here, here, and here in these amounts. Eric took Big Country's calculations and cross checked them with the technical manual only to find the young soldier completely correct in all respects. As the deployment progressed, the leadership took Jeremy's word on these matters and stopped double-checking him. He proved himself a master in his craft.

SSG Pollack's recollection then took him back to the time when they trained Iraqi police. At the bottom of the hill, a group of Iraqi children played regularly. A little girl from this group always wore a bucket on her head like a helmet. Not knowing her name, the U.S. soldiers simply called her *Buckethead*. As they left the training site one day and went down the hill, Jeremy stopped and declared, "It's time to have some fun!" He began to play with the children, kicking around a soccer ball with Buckethead and two other Iraqi kids. He picked two of them up under each arm, laughed, and had a great time in the midst of war. He always knew how to lighten the mood no matter what the circumstances, always wanting to make the most of life.

The other soldiers joined in, playing with the children for an hour of laughter, smiling, and having fun. That day, Jeremy made a positive impact on the life of those children. With all the pain and suffering that those kids experienced daily in a war-torn country and being told that American soldiers were monsters, they learned otherwise firsthand as they played with the U.S. soldiers. This may have changed their view of Americans. Jeremy had a big heart and wanted to make everybody happy regardless of any cultural divide.

Many years later after a second deployment to Iraq, Eric received a medical retirement on August 31, 2012, for PTSD, TBI, and a few physical injuries. He didn't want to leave the Army and fought the discharge unsuccessfully. Eric left active duty extremely disgruntled, taking a lot of prescription medication. Upon returning to civilian life, he tried his hand at farming in the Carolinas. However, he wasn't his usual self. Feeling a profound sense of dissatisfaction there, he bought property in Kentucky where he happily worked on the land and grew life from the earth with his bare hands ever since. Married with three children, he found solace in working the land. Living off his military pension, he also used the crops and livestock to feed his family.

After about eighteen months, he realized how much he missed his brothers-in-arms and subsequently got on Facebook to reconnect with them. He then discovered that Big Country only lived a few hours away. Jeremy spent Labor Day weekend with Eric and his family. Even though they hadn't seen each other for ten years, when Big Country arrived, they picked up right where they left off as if they never parted. Unfortunately, during their conversation, Eric discerned that Jeremy wasn't doing very well. In typical Jeremy fashion, he put the consideration of others first. He brought all of his guitars to entertain everyone else. He even sat down and played the guitar with Eric's daughter. Eric and Big Country talked and smoked until three in the morning. Then Jeremy played a song by the rock band Tool called *46 and 2*. He had broken it down and explained what each part meant to him personally and played it for Eric. Even today, Eric remembered that moment like yesterday because it touched his soul. Reconnecting with Big Country helped Eric tremendously.

Every day Eric dealt with hypervigilance and nightmares. He dreamed of Iraq four or five times a week. Whenever he closed his eyes, he saw that country and the war. To counter this, he always tried to remember and focus on the good things from that time. Despite all these challenges and unfortunate outcomes, Eric considered joining the Army the best decision that he ever made in his life. He considered it an honor to have fought in war next to his brothers. He would do it again in a heartbeat to protect any of them. If a helicopter landed in his front yard today, and they said they had a mission to do, Eric would say without hesitation, "Let's go!" The fiery crucible of combat and war bound him to his brothers-in-arms forevermore. Now, their absence made a hole in his current life.

◆◆◆

On Arizona National Guard duty in August 2018, SSG Ritz Sadang received a group messenger notice about Jeremy's dismal situation. Devastated by the news, he requested the rest of the weekend off to travel to Kentucky to see his brother-in-arms. Ritz grew up in Phoenix, Arizona and joined the Army in August 2003 after graduating from high school. This gave him an opportunity to grow up and have experiences unique to his own life, rather than be corralled into the normal flow of high school, college, and then a career. He also chose this route to have time to figure out who he wanted to be. Ritz did basic training at Fort Leonard Wood, Missouri and then reported to Fort Wainwright, Alaska. He deployed to Iraq in 2005 with the 562nd Engineer Company and again in 2008 with the 1st Stryker Brigade Combat Team, 25th Infantry Division. He then left active duty and joined the Army National Guard changing his military occupational skill (MOS) to EOD. Subsequently, he deployed to Kuwait and Jordan. Upon entering civilian life, he worked for his uncle's business conducting checks and maintenance on printing machines.

Assigned to the same platoon, Ritz met Jeremy while at basic training, their respective rooms across the hall from each other. Adjusting to the rigors of military life, Ritz noticed this big dude who always appeared happy and had a big smile and a powerful projecting voice. Everyone liked Jeremy and seemed to gravitate toward him. As the training progressed, Ritz and Jeremy too became friends. By the end of basic, Big Country had befriended everybody. When traveling in the cattle trucks, Jeremy would break out singing cadences, and soon everyone else joined in despite the long, tiring day. Never in a foul mood, Jeremy had the ability to cheer anybody up no matter the situation. People felt welcomed around him because of the kindness that emanated from his genuine heart. This big dude with a big heart would give someone a bear hug, and all stress and grief evaporated. When he saw a fellow soldier down in the dumps, he went out of his way to cheer up such a one. Over the years, Ritz never had or even saw a negative experience with Jeremy. Everything about him always seemed positive.

After basic training, they had the same initial duty station at Fort Wainwright where they trained together, went out drinking afterward, went on fishing trips, and always had a good time. He recalled how Jeremy drank a lot, but it never seemed to affect his quality of work. A one-of-a-kind person, Jeremy made others feel better about themselves no matter the circumstances. Whenever someone complained about the current situation, Jeremy always found a silver lining or bright spot on which to focus. He blessed Ritz's life thus in a thousand little ways, teaching him to always look for the positive. Without fail, Jeremy availed himself to anyone who needed to talk about something. At the end of the day during the Iraqi deployment, they lit a fire pit at their compound, gathered round to sing songs, and drink fake beer while Jeremy played his guitar. They chatted among themselves about anything and everything. This camaraderie forged an unbreakable bond among brothers who shared the same hardships within a land devastated by war.

Ritz talked to Jeremy a few times over the years after they both got out of the Army. They used those rare moments to just catch up on what happened in each other's lives. During the course of his deployments to Iraq, SSG Sadang encountered several IED explosions near him but fortunately didn't sustain TBI. He did, however, suffer from PTSD. Ritz learned, as the days went by, how to manage and in some cases hide the PTSD with which he dealt. PTSD carried a stigma with it, so most veterans didn't want others to know that they had emotional and mental issues. As time progressed, Ritz's nightmares lessened. He did experience some rough spots over the years but focused on the positive things in life and successfully worked his way through them. He also had great love and support from his family.

Arriving in Franklin, Kentucky to see Big Country and show support for the Smith family, Ritz reunited with several of his former Army buddies who also came. He hadn't talked to many of them since 2007. It did his soul good to see them again. They exchanged phone numbers and kept in better contact with each other. Today while traveling for work, Ritz made it a point to meet up with old comrades, sit down for a beer, and catch up on things. Thinking back on his military service, Ritz knew without a doubt that he wouldn't have been able to defend the constitution and its freedoms without the help of his many brothers-in-arms. It took a cohesive unit, teamwork among warriors to accomplish this all-important task. He and his brothers didn't do it for self-recognition but for love of country, for their fellow Americans, and for each other.

♦♦♦

SFC Remi Ramirez grew up in Oceanside, California. He joined the Army in 2003 after graduating from high school because he wanted to earn college benefits. His parents taught him that one had a greater appreciation for the things that one earned, so he chose this route even though his parents offered to pay for his college. A few years into military service, Remi realized that he enjoyed this lifestyle. He loved the constant motivation and opportunity to achieve promotion. After his first four years, he went back to civilian life with the intent of going to college. He also joined a combat engineer company in the California National Guard. As a SGT fresh from active duty and much to his surprise, he had senior NCOs in his guard unit asking him how to properly do demolitions and lead soldiers.

After eight months, Remi concluded that if he ever deployed to a war zone again, he wanted to go with a more knowledgeable active-duty unit rather than the National Guard. Consequently, he reenlisted on active duty but this time as an infantry soldier. During infantry training at Fort Benning, Georgia, the drill SGTs treated him with respect because he bore the same combat patch that they did, having all served previously in Iraq during the same time. Remi even recognized several senior NCO's that he served with back then. During his subsequent career, Remi deployed to Iraq and then Afghanistan.

One day in August 2018, Remi received a missed call from a military comrade. He then noticed a text that said, "Call me back. It's about Big Country." Instantly, angst gripped Remi because such phone notifications preluded bad news. When Remi called back, he received the ominous tidings that he dreaded. The last time that he spoke to Jeremy, Big Country had been doing so much better in life. This news caught everyone by surprise. Upon traveling to Kentucky, Remi got to see many old friends from the 562nd. This did his heart good. Jeremy, over the years, kept in touch with everyone from back then and made them all feel important. Even in his current dire predicament, Jeremy brought people together in a healing kind of way. Even though he couldn't speak directly with Jeremy, Remi could hear his voice offering encouragement and motivation.

Remi thought back to 2003 when he first enlisted and went to basic training at Fort Leonard Wood, Missouri where he met Jeremy Smith who was in the same platoon. Jeremy impressed Remi as a tough young man while also showing a distinct humorous side. Remi recalled one time when Jeremy started whooping and hollering in the shower. When asked what he was doing, Jeremy replied, "I can see my feet!" Big Country had arrived at basic training a little heavy-set. However, he lost enough weight at that point to see his feet when he looked down. Later, Remi noticed how Jeremy stood out among the others in intellect and resilience. Jeremy got ill during basic training but declined to go to sick call because he didn't want to miss any training. At one point, he even threw up blood yet insisted on attending any and all training. He chose to push his body to the limit in order to get as much military knowledge and skill as he could. A timid smile adorned Remi's countenance as he recalled the many impersonations and jokes that Jeremy did. Big Country's humor and genuine care for others revealed this huge guy as a big teddy bear in actuality. He had an innocence that didn't go with his massive body, especially in the Army.

Upon graduation, both soldiers reported to the 562nd Engineer Company in Alaska. The next year, they deployed to Iraq. From day one, great excitement ran throughout the company at the notion of deploying to combat. Upon arriving in Iraq, the soldiers of the 562nd eagerly clamored to do missions outside the wire. Impatient to do the job that they trained for and to serve their country, the soldiers didn't mind the long hours and tough duty. Despite the fact that enemy combatants lurked in the shadows, Remi felt honored to fight against terrorism. He found most days tolerable, except for the ones when someone got killed. Those few days were the worst of his life. To keep up morale, they passed the time drinking, playing the guitar, and singing. Twenty soldiers would gather in a room designed for one person and have a rap battle with the music blaring. Anyone who challenged Jeremy got destroyed.

They primarily conducted route clearance patrols (RCPs) searching for IEDs and keeping the routes open for the flow of troops and supplies. They started with night patrols that quickly transitioned to twenty-four-hour operations. One platoon patrolled the routes during the day, another platoon during the night, and a third platoon performed as a quick reaction force (QRF). Remi remembered when the Stryker vehicle he rode in got blown off a bridge. The 1SG, who decided to go on the mission at the last minute, bumped Jeremy from that vehicle and gave him furlough for the day. Most of the soldiers in the vehicle received serious injuries. Although Jeremy provided encouragement and support to Remi afterward, Big Country carried guilt for having the day off when tragedy struck his brothers.

Anytime anyone got hurt, Jeremy always rendered help or comfort on the scene and afterward. On one mounted patrol, they stopped halfway to refuel and eat. Big Country swapped positions with another soldier for the second leg of the patrol. Jeremy stood over six feet tall, the other soldier only five feet six inches in height. A while later, an IED exploded sending a large piece of shrapnel hurling toward Jeremy. It hit him square in the body armor of his chest. Had Jeremy not traded places with the other soldier, the shrapnel would have taken off the head of his shorter comrade. Jeremy and Remi went on practically all the same patrols for sixteen months looking for IEDs. After a while, they got used to the explosions. As long as nobody got killed or seriously hurt, they just pressed on with life and the war.

After months of high-level operations, as the mission wound down toward the end of the deployment, they found it difficult to switch to a slower pace of working. Upon returning to Fort Wainwright, Alaska, Jeremy got reassigned to the 101st Airborne Division at Fort Campbell, Kentucky, while Remi prepared to end his enlistment and return to civilian life. They kept in touch over the years on Facebook. From time to time, Remi got a random telephone call from Big Country, who simply wanted to say, "I saw this movie and it reminded me of you," or "Hey, man. Just wanted to say that I love you, Brother." Remi knew that Big Country treated all his brothers with such regard. As a drill SGT, Remi often spoke of Big Country when illustrating leadership qualities to raw recruits. They would never know Jeremy Smith in person, but they learned that tough warriors went before them pushing through pain to get the mission done, who knew their jobs left and right to become masters of their craft. That personified Big Country as a soldier.

Remi, as well as the other brothers-in-arms, dropped everything at a moment's notice to go to Jeremy in his time of distress, not because of their tremendous love for him but because of Jeremy's genuine love for them. Compelled by sincere love for people, Big Country had always put others first, touching them deeply and for a lifetime. Remi saw soldiers from the 562nd and the 101st, as well as civilians who knew Jeremy before and after his military service, all coming together to honor Big Country. The situation emotionally devastated so many people because they all admired him so much and considered him such a close friend. Remi pondered all this. He loved Big Country as his own brother and wouldn't hesitate to tell that to anyone. During their deployment to Iraq, Remi knew without a doubt that Jeremy would die for him. That motivated Remi to live up to that standard himself, to have a willingness to lay down his life for a friend.

◆ ◆ ◆

In August 2018 while on break at work, Tony Santos stared in disbelief at a Facebook post concerning Jeremy that greatly upset him. He knew that Jeremy suffered from severe PTSD after his deployments to Iraq and Afghanistan. Tony saw him go from a highly professional soldier to a troubled veteran. Highly active on Facebook years ago, Jeremy seemed scarce lately. After finding out about Big Country's plight, Tony abruptly requested several days off to go to Kentucky. His boss compassionately obliged. Tony's wife expressed support for this as well. Even if they hadn't, Tony was bound and determined to go anyway. When he arrived in Kentucky to show his support for Big Country and his family, he heard firsthand of all the torments and troubles Jeremy experienced since leaving active duty. Tony's heart rent in two. He wrestled with guilt trying to think of what he could have done for Jeremy to prevent this.

Tony attended high school in San Ramon, California. After graduating in 2003, he joined the Army at the age of seventeen, inspired by his grandfather who fought in the Korean War against the spread of communism. Tony felt that the war against terrorism was his generation's burden to bear for the United States of America, his country which he deeply loved. He also thought that military service would offer a good place to start adulthood until he figured out what he wanted to do in life. In August 2003, he went to Fort Leonard Wood for basic training. From there, he reported to the 562nd Engineer Company at Fort Wainwright, Alaska.

Tony recalled the first time he met Jeremy. While cleaning the third floor of the barracks, he saw this giant, mountain of a man playing the guitar loudly. Charisma emanated from his persona. When they made eye contact, Tony saw a look in Jeremy's eyes that conveyed genuine concern for others. Jeremy wanted to know about other people. He made them feel special by drawing out of them their unique talents, value, and worth. Tony perceived Jeremy as a person who was automatically a friend to others. That put him at ease when around this hulking warrior of a man. As Tony pondered his memories of Big Country, they always seemed to involve Jeremy's guitar. They spent hours singing army cadences and making up engineer songs, as well as songs about girls back home. Those times filled Tony with a profound sense of camaraderie.

Tony thought back to when they conducted training. Jeremy trained with such intensity that it became apparent to Tony that Big Country personified the phrase *no better friend, no greater enemy*. Nobody took training or duty as seriously as Jeremy, yet he would be the first one to crack a joke and lighten the mood during tough times. He had a knack for injecting the right humor at the right time. He was the first to give you the shirt off his back. If you struggled during a road march, he would lighten your load and carry some of your burden even though he labored too under his own burden. He trained hard in order to be the most devastating warrior against the enemy. Yet, he had the biggest heart and love for his friends. Jeremy inspired Tony to be the best person he could. Even today, Tony's past experiences with Jeremy inspired him daily.

A smile pushed its way onto Tony's countenance as he remembered the time during training at Fort Lewis, Washington when Jeremy teased the brand-new privates in the barracks. Wearing only shorts, combat boots, and a boonie hat, he harassed the newbies while speaking in an Australian accent. He had everyone busting at the seams with laughter. During long road marches, Jeremy initiated the singing of cadences to divert others from complaining hours into the endeavor. Jeremy taught Tony that one could bring light and humor into any situation to make things better no matter what the circumstances. Big Country inspired him to strive for that attitude in life.

During the deployment to Iraq in 2005, Tony participated in a multitude of route and building clearance patrols, where they blew up IEDs and returned fire upon enemy combatants. Tony recalled the time while on dismounted patrol when some local youths heaved a cinder block from atop a structure onto Jeremy's head. He took it like a champ, never whiny or showing any sign of weakness. He made sure nobody fired upon those teenagers. When they got back to base, Jeremy sat down and wrote a song about it. He strummed the guitar, sang a few humorous verses, and then strummed some more. One day, well into the deployment, some Iraqi children approached Tony. He began to hand out candy to them which brought unspeakable joy to their demeanor in the midst of poverty. Suddenly Tony felt a positive sensation in his heart. He did something to bless humanity in the midst of war and its devastation, resulting in an epiphany that he would never forget. He realized that he could do some good while in a world of destruction. In that moment, he recognized how blessed he was to grow up in America.

The news of Jeremy's current disposition reminded Tony of two devastating events that occurred during that deployment. The first was the day that SPC Boehmer and SGT Morningstar died. That afternoon, the leadership gathered everyone together and informed them that 1st Platoon hit an IED which instantly killed these two valiant soldiers. Upon hearing this, grief struck Tony as he remembered just talking to them that morning. Later, Tony got promoted to SGT and took over SGT Morningstar's team. Even then, he could see how this tragedy deeply grieved these soldiers still.

The other event involved a man named SSG Luckey with whom Tony had developed a strong bond. Before deployment, he went to SSG Luckey's house for cookouts. Everyone adored SSG Luckey's wife who was eight months pregnant. SSG Luckey had just bought her a beautiful new ring prior to going overseas. While deployed in Iraq, Tony and SSG Luckey worked out daily in the gym. SSG Luckey planned to try out for special forces after they got back to the USA. A competent and caring leader, SSG Luckey just seemed to have it all together, a good head on his shoulders, strong faith, and physically fit. One day, Tony had duty in the TOC. He heard over the radio that the unit sustained a wounded soldier. Before long, the word went out that if anyone wanted to say goodbye to SSG Luckey, they better report to the combat support hospital (CSH) asap.

Upon arriving, Tony saw his friend and revered soldier unloaded from the Stryker vehicle and carried into the hospital. Observing the depth of despair that gripped SSG Luckey's soldiers as they escorted the body into the hospital, Tony and a few others volunteered to clean the blood and brain matter from the interior of the vehicle. This was one of the hardest things Tony ever had to do. Afterward, he went inside to pay his last respects. One of the most surreal moments of his life, Tony stood there observing the listless body of his friend on the gurney. A gauze bandage hugged the wounded head of this well-tanned, physically ripped yet lifeless body. Tony deemed this the ultimate injustice. This particular man deserved to live a long and happy life if anyone ever did.

Tony left active duty in 2007 after fighting in the Iraq War and fulfilling his enlistment. He then served two years in the Army Reserve before ending his military service. He went to college and earned a nursing degree. He now worked in the trauma unit of a hospital emergency room and happily married his high school sweetheart raising their three children. The mental and emotional impact of combat hit Tony in waves. He had seasons of healthy living mixed with seasons of depression and issues with TBI such as headaches, insomnia, nightmares, and hypervigilance. As the years passed, the severity of these torments diminished. Through it all, his wife had been an amazing angel of support, his light in the darkness. Having a job that he loved in which he helped others made him feel valuable when tough times hit.

Tony remembered all the good times he had hanging out with Big Country during the years when they both served their country in the 562nd. They joked around, laughed, and talked about girls. Tony had nothing but fond memories of Big Country. Jeremy made everyone feel special. He was one of the cords that bound them all together in brotherhood and camaraderie. Tony felt blessed to have known him.

♦♦♦

When SSG Russell Laws heard about Jeremy's plight, he drove up to Franklin, Kentucky from Phoenix City, Alabama with SFC Remi Ramirez who was stationed nearby at Fort Benning, Georgia, to see their beloved comrade. Russell grew up in Mays Landing, New Jersey. After graduating from high school, he joined the Army, something he had wanted to do ever since grade school. As a kid, he played army-like games with makeshift guns. He considered it an honor to do his duty on behalf of his country. This notion always welled up pride within him because he viewed it as a noble cause bigger than himself. He also longed for the adventure of participating in military missions such as patrolling. August 2003, He went to basic training at Fort Leonard Wood, Missouri and became a combat engineer. From there he went to Fort Wainwright, Alaska.

Russell reported to the 562nd Engineer Company in January 2004, where he met Jeremy, a large country-fed young man who bore the name Big Country. Over time, Jeremy proved himself completely reliable, trustworthy, and good in Russell's eyes. While training at Fort Lewis, Washington in preparation for deployment to Iraq, they hung out and drank after hours. Jeremy loved Wild Turkey whiskey. The 562nd was the most cohesive unit in which Russell had ever served. The intense training during the day and the camaraderie after hours forged an unbreakable brotherhood between the soldiers, a bond that was only strengthened by combat.

Russell remembered Big Country as an easy-going guy who loved to play his guitar. Upon first meeting, Jeremy instantly made a positive impression. He could make a song about anybody or anything at any time. Russell never recalled seeing Jeremy in a bad mood. If he ever was, he never showed it or took it out on anyone. Even on his worst day, Jeremy outshined most people on their best day. Twice the size of Russell, Jeremy would wrestle him, always making sure that his smaller friend never got hurt. Russell always knew that if Jeremy really wanted, he could pulverize him at any time. Russell recalled a time when he had been drinking and messing around. He jumped on Jeremy trying to wrestle him to the ground. Jeremy could have easily flattened him but instead fell to the ground, yielded, and proclaimed Russell the victor. Most of the time, though, when people tried to best Jeremy, he gently yet decisively put them in their place.

Russell thought about their deployment to Iraq in 2005. When a Stryker vehicle in 1st Platoon hit an IED, the blast tore apart the back of the armored vehicle like a tin can. As a result, SGT Morningstar and SPC Boehmer were instantly killed. This emotionally impacted the entire company but hit 1st Platoon the hardest. This tragedy psychologically wounded Jeremy severely, because he greatly admired and cared about those two soldiers. With that incident, the 562nd had a sober realization that this war was real and for keeps. While on this deployment, many soldiers took an emotional beating, especially Jeremy, because of the IED blast that killed SGT Morningstar and SPC Boehmer, the sniper shot killing SSG Luckey, and a Stryker vehicle getting blown off a bridge seriously injuring several soldiers.

Toward the end of the deployment, the 562nd started conducting RCPs with Iraqi soldiers. The Iraqi leadership took this opportunity seriously and wanted to glean as much experience and knowledge from the American soldiers as possible. However, the Iraqi enlisted soldiers didn't share that same sentiment. They often fell asleep during the patrols and stole items from the U.S. soldiers' ruck sacks. On one occasion at the end of a patrol, Jeremy saw a bulge in an Iraqi soldier's pocket and questioned him about it. That soldier replied with harsh words and drew a knife on Big Country. Then the American soldiers began to yell at him in English, prompting all the Iraqi soldiers to yell back at the Americans in Arabic. Fortunately, cooler heads prevailed and averted a serious incident. The Iraqi leadership did an investigation and punished that particular soldier who wielded the blade.

Russell served over thirteen years in the military, having deployed twice to Iraq and then once to Afghanistan as an infantry soldier. He got out in 2016 because he felt that the Army had changed for the worse, was now married with children, and believed he could provide a better living for them in civilian life. He subsequently lived in Alabama where he owned real estate. A few years later, Russell read about Jeremy's heroics during an Afghanistan deployment in a *Stars and Stripes* article. He was immensely proud of him for putting his life on the line to protect others. When Russell arrived in Franklin to honor his beloved friend, he reunited with soldiers that he hadn't seen in over ten years. He marveled pleasantly at the number of brothers-in-arms that dropped everything and came to support Jeremy and the Smith family, but he wasn't surprised that so many did.

◆◆◆

At SSG Luckey's final roll call memorial service, a pair of combat boots neatly sat in a forty-five-degree angle at the base of an inverted M4 rifle with a camouflaged helmet resting upon the stock of the weapon. The unit's 1SG then began to call out the rank and name of each soldier in SSG Luckey's platoon. In response, each soldier sharply replied, "Present, 1SG." The senior NCO then called out, "SSG Luckey." A hush followed. The 1SG called out again, "SSG Bryan Luckey." An eerie silence ensued. The 1SG called out one final time, "SSG Bryan C. Luckey." The playing of taps somberly followed the emotive stillness.

SGT Jeremy Smith then got up, walked to the front of the gathering, and gave this solemn address:

> There are no words to describe the caliber of man that SSG Luckey was. A devout Christian, he lived what he believed. It's hard to think about his being gone. Our deepest sympathies, as well as our hearts, go out to his family, his wife, and his unborn child. SSG Luckey was one of the most dedicated and hardcore men that I ever saw. He and I used to talk about dropping our Special Forces application packets together as soon as we got back from Iraq. We'd always ask each other what we were doing for PT and how far the other intended to run. There was no challenge too great for him. He was the type of man that you wanted to follow because of the example he set. When I think about being a sapper and being hardcore, I think about him.
>
> He was a modest man that didn't boast over his accomplishments, an unwavering motivation, who always had a smile on his face. He was always there if you needed to talk. If you didn't know how to do something, he was always willing to teach. He

took pride in his position and was an outstanding noncommissioned officer. You could tell that his soldiers looked up to him,
respected him, and loved him like a brother. The worst thing
that I ever heard anyone say about SSG Luckey was that he was
just awesome. He always did his best to keep the mission in perspective and never become complacent.

He had a warrior's heart through and through and believed
in what we are doing here. He had a true desire to help the
people of Iraq. At times, the anger that some of us felt towards
the terrorists clouded our perspective towards all the Iraqis
in general. Never did I hear him speak that way. It was always
about getting the bad guys. Anytime anyone spoke negatively
toward the people of the country as a whole, he'd always put
out a perspective that would slice through the fog and help you
focus. He had a pure heart and an unflinching desire to serve his
country. He made the ultimate sacrifice. No matter how tragic
the loss, no matter how big of a hole it's left in the hearts of those
that knew him, it was a sacrifice that he was willing to proudly
make. They don't make finer men than SSG Luckey. I'm sure
those that knew him would agree.

To his unborn child: your father was one of the greatest men
I have ever met in my life. The world is a lesser place without
him. I'm so deeply sorry that you won't get the chance to know
him. Those of us that did know him miss him terribly but take
comfort in knowing that he's smiling down upon us from above.
SSG Luckey, the epitome of what a sapper should be, a leader, a
teacher, motivated, always had a listening ear or a helping hand
for whomever needed it. We'll miss you always, man. We hope
to see you when our time on earth is done. Until then, *sappers
lead the way!*

◆ ◆ ◆

SGT Jordan Stransky quietly gazed at his best friend Jeremy. It reminded
him of the time when he, himself, spent six months in the TBI clinic because
of wounds sustained during an explosion on the battlefield in 2013. Since he
didn't lose any limbs or sustain any noticeable physical damage to his body,
people often rejoiced that he made it back safe and sound. Unfortunately,
reality held a different truth. SGT Stransky always replied, "Even with amazing prosthetic technology, we can't replace the human brain. We can replace
an arm or a leg with a prosthetic limb, but combat veterans will always have
those memories of war and combat ingrained in them for life." Regrettably,
most nonmilitary people don't comprehend this.

Assigned in 2006 to the same unit as Jeremy, Company A, Special Troops Battalion, 101st Airborne Division, Fort Campbell, Kentucky, Jordan, a motor transport operator, didn't glean a good first impression of him. Shortly after Jeremy had taken charge of a squad, one of his soldiers didn't follow instructions. Jeremy loudly proclaimed to that soldier, "We are going to have SGT Smith time!" He took the wayward soldier outside and smoked him with a multitude of push-ups. Upon witnessing this, Jordan concluded Jeremy to be a loud, obnoxious, and cocky bully, an intimidating and massive guy who overreacted and jumped to conclusions.

For Jeremy's part, he also refused to accept Jordan as a friend at first, even though his gut instinct told him that he would be a solid comrade. Jordan reminded him of one of his fellow soldiers who died during the 2005 deployment to Iraq. Jeremy didn't want to make friends with Jordan lest he experience another loss of a close brother. At this point in his life, Jeremy purposely kept people at a distance when he first met them, still sorting out how to deal with the grief of losing a brother-in-arms. Eventually, however, fate demanded an unbreakable bond of brotherhood between the two soldiers.

Jordan, at that time, had bought a house and asked several of his fellow soldiers if they would help him move into it. Literally everyone replied that they couldn't. While contemplating the grim fact that he would have to spend money hiring movers, Jordan noticed a large figure approach. Looking up, he saw Jeremy standing there glaring down at him, all 255 pounds of defined, chiseled muscle standing six feet two inches tall like a brick house. Intimidated, Jordan blankly stared up at the hulking figure hovering over him. With a deep, commanding voice, Jeremy demanded, "Did I hear you ask some of the other guys for help moving into your new house?" Before Jordan could explain that everyone declined, Jeremy insisted on helping. After fruitlessly asking several friends for help, the guy whom Jordan judged harshly had volunteered to assist. Subsequently, a few other soldiers also agreed to help.

They spent the day eating pizza, drinking beer, and moving furniture. Jordan watched in astonishment as Jeremy single-handedly picked up a refrigerator and carried it into the garage. Jordan thought, *Wow, this dude's strength is pretty amazing!* At that point, Jordan began to discern the deep humanitarian depth of this young man who loomed larger than life. Deep down, Jeremy's genuine concern for others matched his physical stature. Jordan soon recognized that underneath the gruff demeanor resided a big teddy bear. The two of them became good friends. Jordan began to call Jeremy *Big Country*. Their shared military experience, especially in a war zone, forged an indestructible ligature of camaraderie between them. They hung out together constantly, to the point where Jordan spent just as much time with Big Country as he did with his wife and children, who referred to Jeremy as *Uncle J.* They all just clicked. Every weekend the two soldiers gulped down brew and raised hell. A weekly ritual, Big Country would buy pizza and go over to Jordan's house, where they drank beer and talked about previous deployments and army life. They went to gun stores and traveled to different places together. They took Jeremy's truck out into the countryside and seized the day mudding. They spent Christmas, Thanksgiving, and social events together and attended the children's ball games. Big Country became a true brother to Jordan.

The night that Jordan's father died, Big Country was the first person that Jordan called to express his grief. A few days later, Jordan encountered a problem with the insurance company. As a result, he had no money for which to give his dad a suitable funeral. Jeremy asked how much money he needed. Jordan hesitated to tell him, not wanting to burden others with his problem. Seeing the obvious angst upon his friend, Jeremy sternly demanded an answer to the question. Jordan relented and stated that he needed five thousand dollars. Later, Big Country returned and tossed the money on Jordan's lap saying, "Don't you ever pay me back! I don't want you to return the money. This is brothers helping brothers. Besides, it's only money. I'll make more." Through the years, Jordan heard Jeremy say that a hundred times over. To him it was simply money. He didn't care because he could always make more. He just wanted to see people happy. Jordan experienced firsthand the unconditional love that dwelled within Jeremy, demonstrated daily by a myriad of sincere acts of friendship and highlighted by monumental acts of kindness from time to time, things that the average person simply didn't do for others.

Among humanity, many people would pledge their help if times of trouble arose, but few ever followed through with this promise, not so with Big Country who always came through. If someone had the fortune of earning Jeremy's friendship, that person definitely had a trusted comrade on his side in any fight. Forever grateful to Big Country, Jordan wondered how he could ever repay him. A few years later, Jeremy found himself in a tight spot financially and needed some quick cash. Yet, he refused to ask for help. When Jordan found out, he sold his truck, took out a small loan, and had the biggest fight of his marriage. However, how could he not repay Big Country's act of kindness when his father died?

A day came in March 2008 when Jordan and Jeremy received orders to deploy for fifteen months to Afghanistan. Even though they had trained respectively as combat engineer and transportation soldiers, the unit got assigned to the infantry as a security detachment. Jordan never drove a truck while there. Rather, they spent most of their time in the Hindu Kush Mountains of northeast Afghanistan conducting infantry missions in various towns and villages in temperature as low as fifteen degrees Fahrenheit in the winter and as high as one hundred degrees in the summer. The arid climate accentuated the dry, dusty landscape which sported rocky ridges, strong winds, and even dust storms. They performed numerous patrols for reconnaissance, a show of force to deter enemy activity, and to locate booby-trapped buildings and IEDs in the roads. They also did key-leader engagements to see how they could assist the local populous.

This continuous isolation from the main base wrought an unshakable comradeship between all the soldiers in the unit as they watched each other's back, safeguarding one another. Consequently, a permanent tie of love and trust developed among the soldiers in that unit. Protecting and encouraging each other in the midst of constant danger, they truly became a genuine family. When the unit got into a hostile situation, everyone looked to Big Country for guidance and encouragement. He became the person that they clung to when things got tough. He knew everything, a walking book, and could read a manual on shape charges and remember every detail about the subject. Not only massive in size, but he also kept his composure so well in harrowing situations.

While on patrol near the village of Dandar in the Laghman Province, they received a report of a weapons cache hidden in a small group of homes high atop a rocky mountainside. The soldiers labored up the steep slope under the weight of seventy pounds of battle armor, weapons, and gear, while the heat and dust choked them. Upon ascending the heights, Jordan positioned himself right around the corner from an alleged booby-trapped house while Jeremy investigated for house-borne explosive devices. Entering through a window, Jeremy noticed a line attached to a door and leading to a hand grenade. He also discerned a piece of wood on the floor to be a pressure plate for a bomb. Big Country resolutely insisted that everyone back off and asked Jordan to beckon two Air Force EOD technicians from the bottom of the hill. Jordan hastened down the slope to retrieve the techs.

Upon their return, the two techs began to negotiate the traps, as Jeremy cautiously straddled the pressure plate. Despite Jeremy's vigilant efforts, one of the techs inadvertently nudged the wooden slat prompting a blasting cap, connected to a 155 mm artillery round, to detonate with a loud *pop!* Without hesitation, Big Country literally picked up each Air Force tech and threw them out the window, he, himself, diving out behind them. Fortunately, the 155 mm round didn't explode. However, as Big Country tumbled uncontrollably down the rocky slope, a heavy rock toppled forcibly upon Jeremy's hand, severing a finger with its jagged edge. Shortly thereafter, two

A-10 Warthogs swooped in and destroyed the house, while a medevac helicopter took Big Country to a field hospital. As he mounted the evac chopper, he bemoaned the fact that he may never play the guitar well ever again. The surgeon at the hospital intended to amputate Jeremy's finger at the first knuckle. Jeremy begged him not to; playing the guitar meant that much to him. Finally, the surgeon capitulated and sewed his finger back together, making no promises that it would take. Fortunately for Jeremy, it did.

During this deployment, Ultimate Fighting Championship (UFC) fighters visited the troops in conjunction with the United Service Organizations (USO). One of the fighters, well known internationally, excused himself to the latrine. A few minutes later, Jeremy himself went to the latrine. Because only a bath curtain separated the commodes, Big Country accidentally walked in on the UFC fighter. He then proceeded to have a full-blown conversation with this international celebrity while the man sat there doing his business. Escapades like this were typical for Jeremy, a man with a great sense of humor. One time while hanging out at Jordan's house, they decided to go to McDonald's for some food. Jordan's wife, who stood four feet seven inches tall, drove. But before leaving, Big Country somehow squeezed into her pink bathrobe. There he stood at the restaurant counter ordering his food in a cowboy hat with a petite pink bathrobe over his clothes. The employees couldn't restrain themselves as they erupted in a chorus of laughter.

After they both left the military, Jordan and Jeremy stayed in touch by texting each other daily just to make sure all was well with the other. Their deep brotherhood compelled them to communicate with each other more than they did with blood relatives. Big Country would go out to eastern Kentucky and visit for a week with Jordan and his family. When he wrestled with the dark place, Jordan took him to the Appalachian Mountains to revive his spirit. There they listened to music and shared how the song spoke to one another's soul. Jeremy began to notice that Jordan struggled emotionally due to his TBI and combat experience. Angst would devour him when he heard loud noises, compelling memories of combat to flood his mind. Knowing from personal experience that music was good therapy, Jeremy encouraged and taught Jordan to play the guitar. From that juncture on, music became a soothing outlet for Jordan, a positive, artistic venue that declared to him that life had a lot of good things to offer despite the despair. Jordan embraced it wholeheartedly. He did his best to play guitar as well as his friend Big Country. This changed Jordan's outlook on the world and literally saved his life.

Jordan developed such admiration, confidence, and trust in Jeremy that he honestly believed if he were on the other side of the globe and his car broke down, Big Country would be on the next flight headed that way.

Gazing at his best friend quietly lying there, great appreciation welled up in Jordan's heart for the other significant person in his life. A stalwart pillar of support throughout the troublesome years, his wife poured out unending love, patience, and support for him. He didn't know what he would do without her, especially now.

♦♦♦

Throughout history, warriors have chosen to fight beside comrades in the face of great odds rather than flee to safety. SPC Jacob Mygatt pondered this over and over in his mind after receiving the grim news about his brother-in-arms, Jeremy Smith. Jacob grew up in Dayton, Ohio. Inspired by his dad's service in the Navy and by other relatives who served in the military, Jacob joined the Army in 2006. He considered it a chance to grow and learn, as well as to serve his country in time of war. He viewed it as an opportunity to fight for those who couldn't fight for themselves and to participate in something bigger than himself. He saw himself as part of a solution fighting evil in the world. Consequently, he went to Fort Benning, Georgia for basic training in August of that year. He then spent a year in Korea after which he joined the 101st Airborne Division at Fort Campbell, Kentucky that had already deployed to Afghanistan when he arrived. Upon completing in-processing, he joined his unit overseas. Shortly after returning to the states, Jacob completed his enlistment and pursued a civilian career. He currently worked in concrete sales for the construction industry.

Jacob had talked with and texted Jeremy for three hours the night before his mishap. Their conversation continued into the wee hours of Thursday morning. Jacob discerned that Jeremy currently dwelled in a bad place emotionally. He tried to draw out what bothered Big Country. Jeremy expressed concern about an important medical appointment that he had the following Monday that scared him. Jacob offered to drive down from Wisconsin the day before the appointment and accompany Jeremy to the medical clinic, but Jeremy declined his gesture not wanting him to go through all that trouble on his account. Jacob called and texted several times later that day with no answer. He tried again on Friday as well. Later that night, Jacob got a call from another army buddy who informed him of Jeremy's situation. Jacob went outside, sat on the deck, and stared off into space in disbelief. Words couldn't express the depth of his grief. Devastated by the news, Jacob traveled to Kentucky to show his support for Big Country and his family.

During the trip, a myriad of memories about their military service raced undaunted through Jacob's mind. He thought about his first combat deployment to Afghanistan and the first time that he met Big Country. In

March 2008 at the age of twenty-two, Jacob held the rank of private first class (PFC) with no combat experience under his belt. In the Army for less than two years, he had spent his time mostly in Korea doing infantry training. Theoretically, he knew how to fight battles but had no real-time combat. Jacob remembered the moment that he stepped off the plane at Bagram Air Base. The abrupt blast of fierce wind from the surrounding mountains smacked his face, officially greeting him to the War in Afghanistan. During in-processing, thoughts of family, friends, home, and combat bombarded his mind. The epiphany that he could die in war became a harsh reality to him at that moment. He struggled to hide the terror that swirled within him. He tried to focus on the opportunity to finally use the infantry weapons and tactics that he learned.

A short while later, Jacob and a few other soldiers got designated to join Alpha Company, Special Troops Battalion, also known as the *Slayers*. Comprised of soldiers with different military skills, Alpha Company had a staunch reputation in combat, always ready and willing to confront the enemy. Here, Jacob met one of the fiercest slayers of all, SGT Jeremy Smith, his new team leader. A Paul-Bunyan-sized man with a loud voice and a strong and confident demeanor, he carried himself in a way that demanded respect yet came across humbly. Everyone called him Big Country, and SGT Smith lived up to that moniker. With bright red hair, he stood over six feet tall and had arms the size of Jacob's thighs. SGT Smith took Jacob to his living quarters and directed, "Put your gear up quickly and meet me outside asap."

Jacob hastily threw his ruck sack and duffel bag down next to his rack and dashed outside. Upon confronting SGT Smith, he noticed a familiar yet intimidating look in the SGT's eye, a look that said, "I'm going to thoroughly savor what's about to happen!" Jacob knew that SGT Smith was about to scuff him up and enjoy every minute of it. Glowering at him with a smirk, SGT Smith declared, "So, you're a big tough infantry guy, huh? You think that makes you special? Well stud, let's see how tough you really are!"

Jacob thought to himself, *Oh no, this is going to be bad!* SGT Smith proceeded to have Jacob run sprints in between push-ups, mountain climbers, and flutter kicks. Within minutes, he felt like vomiting. After thirty minutes, which felt like hours, Jacob questioned the prudence of his joining the Army. He just wanted to roll over and die. Exhausted and struggling to catch his breath, Jacob hoped that the current reprieve meant that the scuffing ended. However, SGT Smith called for a crowd to gather round and proceeded to challenge Jacob to combatives in the gravel until one of them tapped out. Combatives consisted of hand-to-hand combat, utilizing wrestling, boxing, and other fighting styles. When one of the other NCOs gave the signal to start, Jeremy grabbed Jacob much like a bear would grab a hold of a helpless fawn and mercilessly sling it around before devouring it. Jacob felt like helpless prey but fought back against his daunting predator as best he could. After several arm bars, leg locks, and a choke hold, SGT Smith had Jacob powerlessly in his control.

Recognizing the futility of further resistance, Jacob attempted to tap out as everything faded to black. A moment later, he regained consciousness lying on his back with a bunch of other guys standing over him laughing. Pulling the young soldier to his feet, Big Country whispered in his ear, "As long as you're on my team, you will never quit; you will never back down from a fight. You don't quit on me, and I won't quit on you. Got it?" At that moment, Jacob realized that he would come to admire and respect Jeremy as a leader, a man, and later a friend. He knew that once he proved himself trustworthy to Big Country that they would become family for life.

Over the next year, Jacob and Jeremy spent much of their time on the same missions. Big Country was one of a handful of people in Jacob's life that made a deep impact upon the young man. Jeremy had an innate magnetism that compelled people to want to be around him. He could make someone laugh heartily with just a quick glance. He always had a comeback for anything that anyone said and could fire back a comment off the top of his head without missing a beat. His quick wit went beyond humor. Whenever something happened on the battlefield, no matter how perilous the situation, Jeremy always knew exactly what to do. Not only could he think quicker on his feet than most, he also did so with the safety of others in mind first. The proverbial guy who jumped on a grenade to protect others, Jeremy never put himself foremost. Even when it came to the little things such as picking a meal ready-to-eat (MRE), he let everyone else go first and then picked one out for himself from what was left. Tired, dirty, and hungry, the rest of them argued over who got what MRE but not Jeremy.

Jacob recalled a particular mission that they did a few hours north of Bagram Air Base, tasked with clearing a cave system and eliminating any possible threats. They took their gun trucks as far as they could before having to dismount and continue down into a wadi on foot. They patrolled through the treacherous, uneven terrain of the dried-out riverbed until they reached the cave system. The shale made for extremely difficult climbing as they arduously ascended the steep rocky inclines. They finally came within thirty feet of an opening at the side of the mountain. Jeremy hoisted Jacob up to a ledge that led to the grotto, then pulled himself up. Upon entering the cave, they discovered two twenty-by-twenty-foot caverns. Jeremy inspected the left while Jacob the right. They both proceeded with extreme caution, looking for trip wires or any other kind of booby traps that might set off an explosion.

Jacob noticed some burned pages of a Koran and a recently extinguished fire. While working his way to the back of the little cavern, Jacob stepped on a small decorative rug that seemed out of place, resulting in a hollow sound under his foot. He slowly reached down and pulled the rug to the side, revealing a sheet of plywood two feet wide by three feet long. Sliding that to the side as well, he saw a bunch of spent shell casings and a handful of AK-47 rounds in a hole about a foot and a half deep. Jacob called for SGT Smith to check it out. They collected up the loose rounds and took pictures. Upon leaving, Jacob stumbled at the entrance of the cave and began to slip over the ledge with a thirty-foot drop. Jeremy quickly dove toward Jacob sliding his legs out from under him, causing him to hit the ground without going over the edge. Unfortunately, Jeremy's momentum carried him over the side, bouncing violently down the cliff and into the wadi below. As quickly as it happened, it ended when Jeremy crashed into a large rock. Jacob rushed down to him as hastily as he could and found him wincing in pain having the wind knocked out of him. Fortunately, Big Country only sustained a large gash on his arm, scratches to the face, a banged-up knee, and sore ribs. Speechless, Jacob admired him for his willingness to sacrifice his welfare to prevent Jacob from tumbling down the cliff.

Jacob pondered another patrol where they spent the night in a defunct psychiatric hospital nestled in the Afghan mountains, something right out of a horror movie. They pulled up to the vacant facility late into the evening, set up perimeter security with their APCs, and established a schedule for guard duty. Upon entering the eerily empty abode, they all felt a strong sense of the willies. Tired and ready to rack out, they wandered the halls of this uncanny institution to look for rooms with beds, no one wanting to sleep solo. Finding a hall that had rooms that held about eight hospital beds each, Jacob selected his. He ended up in the same room as Jeremy, which was always fun but also terrifying because Jeremy loved to mess with guys while asleep. Consequently, Jacob made sure that he didn't fall asleep first. That harrowing honor went to a soldier they called Vandy who began to snooze heartily before most of them even finished offloading their gear.

Jeremy slipped across the room over to Vandy's bed and carefully buckled the wrist and ankle restraints onto the unsuspecting soldier. He then gingerly wheeled the bed into the hallway as most of the other soldiers eagerly followed holding phone cameras ready to record. With a running start, Jeremy hurled Vandy's bed down the long dark hallway and screamed at the top of his lungs. The restrained bewildered soldier awoke shrieking in terror as his bed catapulted down the corridor hitting a doorway. The bed flipped onto its side with a thunderous crash. Jeremy ran down the hall to check on Vandy as everyone else watched and laughed hysterically with flashlights and cameras rolling. Events like this made that deployment tolerable. Jeremy not only knew how to fight and lead but also how to laugh and have a great time amid dark circumstances. Because of this, Jacob not only respected Big Country's rank but also respected him as a leader. He continued to do so even after leaving the Army.

In 2013, Jacob was diagnosed with PTSD. His wife had noticed changes in his behavior and demeanor involving depression and anger issues. He became more distant and introverted, avoiding people and conversations whenever possible. He became anxious, displayed hypervigilance, and suffered insomnia. When he did sleep, he had nightmares. His wife would wake up in the middle of the night to find him crawling along the floor and yelling for medic support. Receiving treatment and prescriptions from the VA curbed these behaviors until they began to subside over time. During this struggle, Jeremy always expressed genuine love and support for Jacob making him feel like he could conquer the world. Jeremy instilled in him the true heart of a warrior, not only in the mountains of Afghanistan but for life. As long as Jacob had breath in his lungs, he would always speak of Big Country with the highest regard. A giant among men, Jeremy etched upon Jacob's heart valuable lessons about life that forever shaped who he became as a man, father, husband, friend, and lover of this great nation he called home.

◆ ◆ ◆

Raised in Denver, Colorado, Captain (CPT) Will Coulter, moved to Fort Payne, Alabama prior to his senior year in high school. While in college, he spoke to a recruiter subsequent to the 9/11 attacks and procured an Army ROTC scholarship. Upon graduating, he immediately entered active duty, went to the Military Police officer basic course, reported to Fort Campbell, Kentucky, and got assigned to the 101st Airborne Division. At this point, he fully expected to deploy to Iraq, which he did in December 2004, where he served as a platoon leader for a year. Upon returning to Fort Campbell, Will served as a company executive officer, as well as in staff positions, and later got promoted to CPT. In 2007 he deployed to Afghanistan were he became the company commander of Alpha Company, Special Troops Battalion. Upon returning to the U.S., he served until 2012 when he left active duty to get a master's degree and pursue a civilian career.

Sitting in his office in Memphis, Will received a phone call from Dan Marques, a combat brother, informing him about Jeremy. This notification deeply grieved his heart. He thought about all his former soldiers that suffered from PTSD after fighting in combat. The news of Jeremy hit him the hardest though. In addition to serving as a highly competent soldier, Big Country was also a great human being, a huge teddy bear of a man toward humanity, who had so much to offer society and life. Will thought it a great travesty that Big Country's life turned out the way that it did. Jeremy of all people deserved better.

Will thought back to his days of the Afghanistan deployment where he first encountered Big Country. Upon assuming command of Alpha Company, Special Troops Battalion in June 2008, CPT Coulter met Jeremy who served as a team leader in the unit. Whether quiet or loud, Big Country stood out among the rest to Will because of his sheer size. To him, Jeremy Smith loomed as a larger-than-life individual in physical size, character, and personality. When reflecting back on the time he spent with Jeremy, Will couldn't recall a single negative thing about him. In fact, Big Country was probably one of the most generous, selfless individuals he had ever met. Jeremy's respect toward people and his willingness to help others stood out to CPT Coulter.

Will quickly discerned that Jeremy would be one of his go-to guys when he needed something done right. Jeremy never hesitated to volunteer for missions, quickly gave credit to fellow comrades, and always took blame for the shortfalls of his soldiers. Big Country quickly established himself, in Will's view, as one of his top performers in the company . Without fail, Jeremy held sway as the largest personality in the room without being the loudest or most talkative. He never demanded attention but with his genuine personality and talents always got it, especially with his guitar strumming abilities. Will thought back to times in their Combat Outpost (COP) after a long patrol, when Jeremy sat in a corner of the courtyard and played his guitar. Soon a majority of the unit huddled around smoking cigarettes and discussing life events. Jeremy created an environment that brought people together because he had a natural talent to draw others.

Assigned to the Bagram Air Base during the Afghanistan deployment, Alpha Company performed many missions out of operating posts in the Kapisa and Parvan Provinces. These assignments involved training Afghan police, counter-rocket-attack patrols, leader engagements, and maintaining vigilance at one of the outposts in their area of operation. Will would rotate accompanying his various platoons while they conducted these missions. Mission types included security, governance by building good relationships with local leaders, and development of local infrastructure. Security patrols took up most of their time. While back at the main base in Bagram, Will made an effort to keep his distance from the enlisted soldiers to give them as much space and time to unwind and relax without their commanding officer. In so doing, he only interacted with Big Country on a professional basis while performing missions.

CPT Coulter's most prominent memory of Jeremy occurred in Spring 2009 when Big Country put the lives of others before his own. On that morning, the unit received a report that enemy personnel had compiled a weapons cache within the company's area of operation. The Afghan Police concluded it a credible threat and requested U.S. support to investigate. A long and rugged road led out to the suspected house, which sat atop a mountain only accessible by foot or air insertion. Elements of Alpha Company arrived at the base of the mountain and set up a security perimeter. With the sun approaching high noon, Will organized a dismounted patrol to trek up to the suspected cache site. Finally reaching the top of the mountain, the patrol entered a small village which seemed to materialize out of nowhere. Will ordered his soldiers to search all of the homes and evacuate any civilians found. The Afghan Police alerted them to a lone home on the edge of a cliff that they suspected housed the cache.

Will tasked Jeremy assisted by an EOD team to investigate the home further. Upon entering the dwelling, the team discovered a small room with a door leading to the cellar. The door appeared suspicious with wires leading to what looked like a grenade. A metal box also sat in front of the door and appeared to contain something. While the EOD team examined the booby-trapped door, Jeremy provided security and shielded them from the metal box. Jeremy requested that CPT Coulter survey and evaluate the situation. Standing on the side of a cliff, Will observed through a window since the small room wouldn't hold all four soldiers safely. Will then received a radio call and stepped to the side to deal with an issue from higher headquarters.

Upon completing the radio call, CPT Coulter turned back toward the window and heard a small explosion like a loud piece of fireworks igniting. As he tried to look inside the house, one of the EOD soldiers dove out. Will saw Jeremy lunge toward the window and then stop suddenly. Big Country abruptly turned and grabbed the other EOD soldier who had tripped and fallen. Jeremy literally picked him up completely off the ground and threw him out the window like a sack of potatoes. Once everyone else was safely out of the house, Jeremy dove out of the window himself. He leaped farther out in an attempt to avoid the EOD soldiers. Consequently, Big Country slid down the cliff a bit causing large rocks to tumble over him. One sharp rock landed on his hand nearly severing a finger. Jeremy calmly stood up and began to dress his wound. He didn't blame or lash out at the EOD team, which tripped the explosive. Instead, he checked to make sure that they were okay. Will immediately called a medevac to take Jeremy to the hospital to save his finger from amputation.

To Will, Jeremy hailed as a one-of-a-kind person who always helped others first and never asked for anything himself. Always a giver, Big Country used only what he needed to survive and nothing more. After Will resigned from the Army, he heard that Jeremy had sustained another more serious injury while again deployed to Afghanistan. This wound caused significant damage to his leg. Unfortunately, at the time, he couldn't get many details on the incident. Will pondered how much more this valiant warrior could take. As a result of this news, a depressed mood glowered at Will for days to come. Thinking upon Big Country's current state, CPT Coulter experienced shock, anger, and sadness all at the same time. Will had lost several friends and soldiers in combat. However, those falling victim to PTSD bothered him most. In those cases, he often wondered if he could have done more to help. Will woefully concluded that Jeremy, the selfless giver, gave everything that he had until he had nothing left to offer.

◆◆◆

Dan Marques enjoyed his civilian life and went about his daily routine when a text message notification on his phone caught his attention. Upon reading the message stating that Big Country had a terrible mishap, extreme grief coupled with mild shock engulfed his being, as he stared at the message in dismay. Dan grew up in Corona, California, went to the United States Military Academy West Point because he wanted to get away from home and challenge himself, and earned a commission as a Military Intelligence officer. Later his battalion commander sent him to Ranger School with the intent of placing him in charge of a specially formed platoon. Upon return, he became platoon leader of the Reaper Platoon, Alpha Company, comprised of soldiers from numerous MOSs designed to perform infantry missions while capitalizing on different skill sets. The battalion affectionately called it the *Frankenstein platoon* because of its odd composition.

Dan's memory whisked him swiftly away on a journey of recollection, depositing him at Fort Campbell, Kentucky at a time when he served as a first lieutenant (1LT). Dan initially met Jeremy in June 2007 after taking charge of this new platoon designed to operate as a quick reaction force to a multitude of scenarios by assembling together the highest quality soldiers from the various military skills in the unit. One of the first enlisted soldiers to join the platoon, Jeremy came from the division engineer's office. 1LT Marques had his doubts about such a unit functioning cohesively and efficiently. After meeting Jeremy and working with him for a few days, he had a more comfortable feeling about the platoon running smoothly, because of Big Country's knowledge and dedication. At the beginning, only a handful of soldiers adorned the platoon. During a formation prepping to do PT outside the company headquarters, Dan came out from a commander's meeting. Jeremy snapped to attention and saluted smartly, prompting the younger soldiers to do the same, even though Dan simply wore shorts and a T-shirt. Jeremy's discipline and military bearing left a lasting impression on Dan. He could tell that Jeremy was a person who always did the right thing even when nobody else watched.

1LT Marques stopped and introduced himself to the young SGT. He had a good feeling that Big Country would become one of the backbone leaders of the platoon, so he assigned him as a team leader. Larger than life, Jeremy had a presence that put a person at ease with a tender, sincere, and genuine persona even though he could smoothly transition into loud, boisterous, and gregarious behavior, a mixture of character traits not often found in one individual. He seemed to have a personality that spanned the entire spectrum, sometimes incredibly quiet and then very vocal. The longer he knew Jeremy, the more he understood him on a deeper level. Jeremy had the ability to hold the undivided interest and attention of others. Dan concluded that Big Country possessed one of the most dynamic, all-encompassing personalities that he had ever met. This made Jeremy a special leader and person.

Jeremy quickly became one of the bedrocks of the platoon and used his influence with other soldiers to set a positive tone. While deployed to Afghanistan, the platoon went days and sometimes weeks without encountering the enemy. Even so, he meticulously made sure that weapons and vehicles were kept clean and functional. He maintained a high level of tactical proficiency in the platoon at all times. Even when everyone else felt confident that they wouldn't make enemy contact on a routine patrol, Big Country constantly drove soldiers to do the right thing and engage in proper tactical behavior. He ensured that everyone did pre-combat checks and knew how to respond to all contingencies by constantly drilling and preparing others. He had the ability to do all this without coming across as an overbearing leader, pushing people to do their best while garnering their respect rather than resentment. Jeremy achieved this by always leading by example. He never asked anyone to do something that he didn't do himself. He was the first one through a door when clearing a room and the first one to expose his position in order to get a better vantage point. Everybody recognized this, so younger soldiers never hesitated to follow his orders. He carried such tremendous credibility because of his behavior and performance that higher-ranking soldiers regularly came to him for advice.

Aside from being an exceptional soldier, Jeremy also provided comic relief, even when he personally had some awfully bad days. Coming off an all-day foot patrol in the Tegab Valley, drenched with sweat, caked in dust, shuffling back to base, Jeremy began to make various impressions that lifted the morale and spirits of his comrades. While the unit cleaned vehicles and equipment after returning to base, he told jokes and cut up. He made his brothers-in-arms feel like part of a family and still human despite their circumstances. A slight smile adorned Dan's face as he recalled the time when his Crohn's Disease flared up while on patrol. He told the driver to pull over somewhere so that he could resolve the issue as discreetly as possible, not wanting to draw attention to himself or the platoon. As the vehicle pulled over and 1LT Marques exited, Jeremy announced jovially on the radio, "Everyone pull security; the Lieutenant is taking a sh-!" Laughter erupted throughout the convoy of armored vehicles. When things seemed their worst, Jeremy seemed at his best tactically as well as comically.

Dan started out as Jeremy's platoon leader for six months. While deployed to Afghanistan, Dan got promoted and became the company executive officer. As a young platoon leader in combat, Dan greatly appreciated having such a stellar SGT in his platoon. Jeremy was the only NCO that had a profound impact on Dan. For the rest of his life, Dan had tried to emulate Jeremy's humility, unwavering commitment to the people around him, and dedication to upholding a standard of excellence especially in keeping others safe. Inherently, Jeremy personally held himself to this standard. Watching Jeremy's leadership performance significantly influenced Dan's leadership style in combat, as well as today in civilian life.

In Afghanistan, 1LT Marques spent time with Big Country just talking, drinking, playing the guitar, and hanging out as twenty-five-year-old guys. But when the situation required it, Jeremy responded with the highest military professionalism. Because of this, Dan could have a friendship with Jeremy while not compromising their professional military relationship. Officers easily interacted with Jeremy on a social basis while still maintaining the professional rank structure; not so with other soldiers because they would take advantage of the friendship and compromise the discipline required for proficient combat operations. Dan never had that concern with Jeremy. This was another attribute that made him such an outstanding soldier. Jeremy befriended officers while recognizing boundaries and rank.

Dan remembered having heart-to-heart conversations with Jeremy about Big Country's previous deployment in Iraq. Jeremy shared with him the details of a firefight in a village where a couple of rooftop positions fired upon them. At that moment Jeremy realized for the first time that no matter what course of action he took, his life could be snuffed out in an instant under such circumstances. This epiphany gave him an overwhelming sense of helplessness during moments of enemy engagement. Ignoring the angst, he performed his duty as trained. During his combat tours, he encountered numerous firefights with the enemy engulfing him in life-and-death scenarios. Dan wondered if this took a heavy toll on Jeremy's psyche since many people perform bravely during a crisis and then succumb afterward to the stress.

Fortunately, the Reaper Platoon only encountered a handful of skirmishes during this Afghanistan deployment. One time at an outpost in the Tegab Valley, while attached to a Special Forces unit assigned to investigate a high value target, they provided security for the special operations soldiers. Late in the afternoon, they departed the outpost, maneuvered through the nearby village, and then cautiously entered a wooded area where an informant lived. The Special Forces talked with the source for a while and finished as the sun began to kiss the western horizon. On the way back, they had to cross an ominous road, hike up a mountainside, and set up their patrol base for the night. Unfortunately, they didn't wait until dark to cross the road and silhouetted their presence in the dusky landscape. As a result, insurgent mortar fire soon descended upon them. The U.S. soldiers quickly scrambled for cover, reorganized, and scoped the land looking for the enemy position in order to call in an airstrike.

Another incident occurred when they left the outpost and drove through a village to patrol the Tegab Valley. They crossed paths with a sister platoon that came in from a patrol. The two platoon leaders stopped to coordinate information. At that point, all was quiet as each platoon continued on its way. A few moments later, the other platoon leader declared over the radio that they made enemy contact resulting in one soldier killed, three wounded, and a disabled vehicle. Dan's platoon had just traveled that stretch of road a few moments earlier. The Reaper Platoon immediately turned around to provide quick reaction support. Jeremy, as truck commander (TC) in charge of his assigned armored vehicle, performed valiantly in setting up security and rendering aid to the wounded. One armored vehicle lay completely upside down damaged by a rocket propelled grenade (RPG) round that had caused the casualties. In a mild state of shock, the soldiers of the sister platoon gathered the remains of their dead SGT as best they could, placed them on a stretcher, draped him with an American flag, and placed him on a Black Hawk helicopter, never to see him again. With tears streaming down their distraught faces, the soldiers who survived saluted as the helicopter departed. One of the worst scenes that Dan had ever seen in his life, this event seared itself into his psyche forever.

Returning to Fort Campbell upon completion of this deployment, the battalion recognized Jeremy for valor, heroism, and selfless service. Dan had the privilege of reading the citation awarding Big Country the Bronze

Star. Afterward, Dan introduced Jeremy to his fiancé, Kelly, emphasizing his bravery and the recognition that he had just received as a war hero. Kelly marveled at his heroics. In response, Jeremy demonstrated uncommon humility, gave credit to the entire unit, and stated that he felt honored to serve in the Army and with this particular group of soldiers. At that moment, Big Country's meekness and introspection overwhelmed CPT Marques. Then Jeremy proceeded to exalt Dan for his leadership. Having the opportunity to talk about himself and his accomplishments, Jeremy chose instead to display humbleness and deferred praise and honor to those around him. By far, he lived his life as a giver rather than a taker. Several years later, Dan's mom posted his picture on Facebook as a tribute during Veterans Day. In response, Jeremy wrote a shining, lengthy commentary extolling Dan's military service. Jeremy eagerly exalted others while never looking for recognition in return.

Everyone had different reactions to the traumas of combat. For Dan, combat gave him a profound appreciation for the tremendously blessed life he had. He returned from war fully recognizing the freedom and liberty he enjoyed as an American and his great fortune to have survived combat. His combat experience made him a stronger, better person who understood how bad things could get and how good a life he currently lived. He fully appreciated how much those who gave the ultimate offering upon the altar of freedom truly sacrificed for him, his family, and all Americans. Sometimes he felt guilty seeing his brothers-in-arms struggle with the aftermath of combat, such as Jeremy. Thinking often about this compelled Dan to strive to live his best, to earn the right to enjoy such a bountiful existence when fate didn't afford others the same. He saw firsthand how fleeting life could be. All the worst days that Dan ever experienced while serving in war ended up making the year from which he matured the most and laid within him a more excellent moral foundation for the rest of his life. Dan would always remember Jeremy as a significant part of this.

♦♦♦

Originally from Allentown, Pennsylvania, 1SG Jason Andrews joined the Army in February 1991 because his mother had recently died at a young age and the Lehigh Valley area offered scarce job opportunities due to a decline in the U.S. steel industry. Upon graduating from basic training at Fort Knox, Kentucky, he spent his military career as an Armor soldier, during which he did combat tours in Bosnia, Iraq, and Afghanistan. Sitting at home now retired from the military, Jason got a message from a brother-in-arms requesting a callback. Upon returning the call, Jason grimaced at hearing of

Jeremy's dire condition. His heart sinking into his gut, Jason wouldn't wish ill upon others, least of all Jeremy, whom he considered the most lovable guy ever, despite being a ferocious warrior. Like so many, he assumed that Jeremy, a great man and bigger than life, would overcome PTSD in due time. With tears welling in his eyes and throat knotting up, a sharp pain pierced Jason's soul as he pondered whether he could have done more to help this valiant hero who once served under his charge.

This grim contemplation devoured and propelled 1SG Andrews back to 2007, when he initially met Big Country in division headquarters at Fort Campbell, Kentucky. Laying eyes upon him for the first time, Jason immediately thought, *Sh-, you're a big fu-!* Later, he marveled at how easily he, a battle-hardened NCO, became deeply fond of Jeremy's gentle-giant persona. Unless the situation required otherwise, Jeremy overflowed with kindness and consideration for others. In time, Jason discovered that Jeremy was a reliable soldier in combat and would become a friend for life. A beleaguered smile adorned Jason's face as he recalled how easily people could talk and laugh with Jeremy. He also remembered how Jeremy was always task and detail oriented despite his easy-going attitude with people. Jason greatly admired Jeremy's openness and genuine care for others. His reliability and selflessness inspired Jason to be a better person himself. Jeremy's larger-than-life persona never overwhelmed his selfless desire to put everyone else first. Regardless of the personal circumstances in which he found himself, Jeremy would drop everything at that moment to help someone else. This willingness to sacrifice his own needs to help others demonstrated Jeremy's true love of brotherhood.

A few months later, the division assigned Jason as the 1SG of Alpha Company, Special Troops Battalion, 101st Airborne Division. He now had 275 soldiers in his charge within a uniquely organized unit that encompassed the division headquarters and included several full-bird colonels and sergeants major. The company also had a multitude of soldiers with different MOSs mixed together in numerous combat platoons, which made cohesion a challenge. However, in the end, this unit bonded together and worked as a smooth-running organization in the war zone thanks to guys like Jeremy who had combat experience. Other soldiers really looked up to him because of his knowledge and his leadership ability. He greatly contributed to mission effectiveness, enhancing the unit's ability to complete missions well and survive in the combat theater. This made Big Country a tremendous asset to the company, other soldiers, and Jason.

Alpha Company deployed to Afghanistan in March 2008 and returned May 2009. Jason soon found that he could trust Jeremy to accomplish any assigned task well. Whenever he needed something done, he knew that he could go to Jeremy to do it properly, relieving Jason of the burden of constantly watching over or following up on the matter. Jeremy always completed his tasks at or above expected standards. It wasn't always a smooth road, however. Early on, 1SG Andrews encountered a myriad of minor discipline issues in the unit. Tired of correcting individual soldiers for their infractions, Jason gathered all the SGTs in the company and scuffed them on a hot day with physical activities on the paved road next to their building. The following day, Jason noticed blisters on Jeremy's hands and inquired. Jeremy replied that the asphalt road from the previous day's scuffing had burned his hands. Feeling bad, Jason asked why he didn't say something then. Big Country gave Jason a confused look and said, "Why? We deserved everything that you dished out yesterday for not enforcing the proper level of discipline in the unit." Jason marveled at his integrity and willingness to take the heat for the actions of his soldiers.

The company leadership rotated going out on assignments with the various platoons. So, 1SG Andrews didn't personally go on every mission that Big Country did. However, when Jason did accompany Jeremy's platoon, they spent days at a time isolated at a small outpost in the mountains. Primarily, major enemy threats came at them from a distance via mortars, rockets, or IEDs—the IEDs being the greatest nemesis. Consequently, elements of Alpha Company didn't get into many firefights on this deployment. Jason learned that a major difference between the Iraqis and the Afghans was that the Iraqis conducted hit and run operations, while the Afghans hit with an IED and then followed it up with a complex ambush, meaning to put up a strong fight. Fortunately for Alpha Company, no such trap happened to them.

During missions, they were objective-focused, but afterward they engaged in camaraderie that wrought a close-knit brotherhood, often buying a goat from a local herder to have a cookout. A spontaneous laugh emerged from deep within Jason's soul as he remembered the three amigos, Jeremy, Jordan Stransky, and Eric Lathrop. When those three got together after-hours doing impersonations or razzing each other, comedy central ensued. Jason unconsciously shook his head in jovial judgment as he recalled Jeremy making light of his combat injury. He had just dived out of a window of a house booby-trapped with explosives and injured his finger. Holding his hand up with the finger pointing in the wrong direction and ignoring the pain, he wiggled his hand a bit, laughed, and inquired loudly, "Hey, Top! What do you suppose is wrong with my hand?" He then proceeded to make jokes about it. For a moment, these recollections engulfed 1SG Andrews in a shroud of comfort, as he once again felt the strong bond of friendship and brotherhood that they all shared back then.

More memories of their deployment flooded 1SG Andrews's mind. When intelligence came in about the location of IEDs or IED cells working in a certain village, their unit air assaulted into remote areas to investigate. Upon insertion, they took the high ground, set up security, and then sent a team into the village to check things out. In addition, their battalion had two provinces in which they did routine patrols. Since soldiers of various military skills such as infantry, transportation, and engineers comprised the unit, they used their different expertise as needed to accomplish missions. Despite the numerous assignments that Jeremy did, he never complained about anything. He kept it all under wraps inside himself and usually dealt with tough situations by using humor.

1SG Andrews recalled one of their first missions when they went to patrol a little village. An inexperienced soldier drove the vehicle in which Jason rode and got it stuck in a canal. They attempted to use another vehicle to dislodge the trapped one, got it embedded in the mud as well, and eventually called for a recovery vehicle. As a result, they spent quite a bit of time at that village. Little by little, more Afghans show up to observe the turmoil. As the day dragged on, the locals became more and more unruly, perhaps because the prolonged presence of Americans might draw attention from the Taliban and result in a mortar or rocket attack. Fortunately, Jeremy had the ability to connect with the local populous and put them at ease. When a situation got tense, Jeremy always kept a cool head about him. He was able to joke with the locals and connect well with the children. In Afghanistan, if the children trusted a particular group of U.S. soldiers, then the adults would give them the benefit of the doubt. If the children didn't trust them, that put the adults on heightened alert. Fortunately, Jeremy had a knack for handling that type of situation.

By the time that they got the vehicles unstuck, about three hundred Afghans had arrived on scene. By interacting with the locals, Jeremy defused any escalation of emotions and attitudes. One villager, highly upset at the situation, arrived yelling at the U.S. soldiers. Through an interpreter, Jeremy got that man to calm down. The locals had a tendency to get mad about anything. If one person got irate prompting another to chime in, it didn't take long before a mob ensued, and the situation turned into total chaos. If they didn't soothe the situation immediately, it would quickly escalate and spiral out of control. Big Country proved himself a great asset in this regard. If a situation began to arise, he quickly interjected to calm things down. At the end of the day, they financially compensated the local populous for any damage done to their village.

Jeremy also possessed amazing analytical skills. He could evaluate a mission and in his after-action report (AAR) point out things that could be done better next time, which others overlooked. Not only that, but he could explain and justify in detail why his observations would increase proficiency. He communicated well, clearly and concisely explaining the why of doing something. This made him a great trainer and earned him the trust and respect of all soldiers. They also endeared him because of his musical talent. When sitting around back at the main base, Jeremy broke out the guitar, started twanging away, and sang to entertain others. He always drew a crowd and lifted the spirits of those around him.

After both Jason and Jeremy departed the military, they stayed in contact quite a bit, sometimes even talking in the predawn hours of the morning. To this day, 1SG Andrews still receives phone calls from his former soldiers, seeking guidance and advice. Jason remembered how Jeremy vented about the injury that he received during his last deployment and some of the struggles that resulted. He also complained about the low-quality treatment that he received from the system. One bad thing about the military, it considered soldiers second-hand when no longer mission-ready. The treatment that Jeremy received at that point greatly diminished his sense of worth and purpose in life. When soldiers no longer seemed useful, the system tended to throw them away. Unfortunately, like most combat veterans dealing with PTSD, Jeremy went above and beyond to assist others in their struggles but didn't do so for himself or even allow others to help him. It was because of the stigma that went with PTSD, a disorder. Who wanted to acknowledge that they had a disorder? The attitude of a soldier was that one endured the pain and drove on. However, at some point, it would catch up with them, as it did Jeremy. With every fiber of his being, 1SG Andrews wished that he had discerned what was really going on inside of Jeremy.

♦♦♦

SFC Nick Smith sat quietly in the room gazing in dismay at his good friend Jeremy Smith. Although not related to each other, they became close comrades over the years. Nick only served with Jeremy in the military for scarcely six months but felt like he knew him forever. Within that short time, Jeremy made a profound impression on him that would last a lifetime. Like Jeremy, Nick loved the Army. His grandfather served in the Korean War, while his aunt served in the Army for twenty-six years. Although admiring both of their service to the country, Nick, as a young man from Urbana, Ohio, initially joined the Army in July 2001 to earn money for college. He then fell in love with the army life and eighteen years later still hadn't gone to college, choosing rather to devote his life to military service for his country.

He learned firsthand that if one had a job that one loved, that person never worked a day in life.

Nick's dad earned a living as a diesel mechanic, a trade that Nick enjoyed too. However, he felt that there had always loomed something larger than himself out there that beckoned him. It turned out to be military service. If people like Nick didn't serve to protect freedom and liberty, then those things would go away. Originally, he joined the Army for himself, but then began to serve in order to protect the rights and blessings of future generations of Americans, a sentiment that he and Jeremy both shared. Nick excelled beyond his military peers, completing air assault and pathfinder training, as well as making SFC in less than nine years, a real natural soldier and leader. Nick deployed to combat in Iraq in 2003, again in 2005, to Afghanistan in 2006, and again in 2010. Regardless of the horrors of combat and his injuries, Nick would serve in the military all over again if he could. Unfortunately, he had a clash with cancer for five years in which at one point the doctor said he had three to eight months to live. Miraculously he prevailed but would receive medical retirement a few years shy of the twenty for which he had hoped.

Sitting there heavyhearted looking at Jeremy, Nick's mind took him back several years to that first day when he arrived at his new unit as a SSG. After a tour as a drill instructor at Fort Jackson, South Carolina, Nick reported for duty in the 2nd Brigade Special Troops Battalion of the 101st Airborne Division at Fort Campbell, Kentucky in January 2010. This unit supported the 1st and 2nd brigades of the 502nd Infantry Regiment. On that particular day, the commander locked down the company. Nobody could go in or out without his or the 1SG's permission because of an epidemic of K2 and Spice synthetic marijuana. Nick called his wife to let her know that he had to stay in the company barracks until the lockdown ended—off to a good start! The 1SG assigned Nick to monitor the doors along with SGT Jeremy Smith. Nick heard several soldiers declare that trying to get out would be futile because SGT Smith guarded the doors. The soldiers had an immense reverence for SGT Smith and refused to try to manipulate their way past him. Nobody would succeed in getting by Big Country. It took three days to completely search the company area to discover and remove the soldiers who dealt the drugs.

Always a first-rate NCO, Jeremy never made his soldiers do anything that he hadn't already done or wouldn't do himself. Being a great person first and foremost himself became the foundation of his success as a leader. His unwavering professional attitude infected the entire unit in a truly positive way. He had an innate ability to turn a bad situation around. Jeremy's demeanor and behavior commanded respect from others as his persona just elicited it naturally. Jeremy could tell soldiers not in his squad to do something, and they did it without hesitation. A natural mentor and teacher for younger people, he didn't have to yell at his soldiers very often. Just letting them know that they disappointed him as their leader convicted them to correct their actions and behavior. Jeremy had a knack for bringing out the best in young soldiers who had attitudes. He saw the potential in all of them and cultivated it with tough love. He had an inborn ability to figure out people and how to reach them.

Jeremy stood as a towering solid mass of two hundred sixty pounds of muscle, whom nobody defied. Nick himself wielded a muscular physic of two hundred forty pounds and was called *Little Smith*. During company runs, the platoon SGT always killed off Jeremy and made the other soldiers carry him back to the company area. They grumbled, "Kill off someone else, not SGT Smith! He's the biggest guy in the company." To which they received the reply, "Oh yeah, he's dead! Now carry him back to the company area."

An excellent shooter, Jeremy was designated a unit marksman with the long-range rifle. He affectionately gave his rifles names. Jeremy always handled adversity quickly, fast, and in a hurry. Because of his proficiency and combat experience, he showed his squad leader many things about leading soldiers effectively in a war zone. At that time, Nick led second squad, while Jeremy assisted with third squad. On the lighter side, Jeremy did great impersonations. He sounded more like Arnold Schwarzenegger than Arnold Schwarzenegger. An avid troubadour, he also gave names to his guitars. Extremely talented, he could pick up a box with guitar strings on it, begin to play, and soon have a crowd around him. He could play most songs by ear from memory when requested. His fellow soldiers listened to him play all night long.

In June 2010, Jeremy deployed to Afghanistan for the second time. During the flight from Kyrgyzstan to Afghanistan, Jeremy chided a young eighteen-year-old supply clerk, inexperienced in life and the military, green as St Patrick's Day. This kid was scared to death sitting in the C-17, white as a ghost. With a mischievous grin, Jeremy coached him, "During the flight, you have to puke on the plane. Oh yeah. It's a rite of passage. You won't be a real soldier if you don't." The others chimed in making mock puking noises. During the intense vertical combat ascent of the plane at takeoff, the young soldier finally puked amid a chorus of laughter from the veteran soldiers.

Their unit had settled into an FOB near Kandahar for only a few weeks when the 82nd Airborne FOB got hit by a truck bomb, which did a lot of damage. The engineers in Jeremy's company were assigned to reinforce the 82nd Airborne base and do a battle damage assessment to determine what assets they would need to make repairs. About eight combat engineers were sent on an advance party ahead of the rest of the unit. They traveled with an Arkansas National Guard engineer unit conducting an RCP for that area. The Arkansas unit assigned them two to four seats in three of the vehicles and rolled out on July 2, 2010, along with a unit of Afghan soldiers. Jeremy rode in a MaxxPro MRAP (Mine Resistant Ambush Protected) vehicle in the middle of the convoy, while Nick rode in the second vehicle from the front.

About twenty kilometers (klicks) from their destination, a Taliban ambush lay in wait to decimate the convoy with RPGs and 80 mm rockets from recoilless rifles, which looked like direct-fire mortars. With an RPG round, the Taliban ambush first hit and disabled the lead vehicle, a Husky mine detector, to create a choke point in the road obstructing the rest of the convoy. Then the enemy hit and disabled the rear vehicle preventing the convoy from turning around and disengaging the kill zone. The Taliban then proceeded to disable eleven of the thirteen vehicles that comprised the convoy. Although disabled, each vehicle's crew-served-weapons gunner immediately engaged the attackers. All of the National Guard vehicles turned toward the enemy firing a heavy deluge of bullets.

Once the ambush commenced, SSG Nick Smith tried to exit the vehicle through the rear ramp, but a heavy rate of enemy fire impacted everywhere. When Nick saw that Jeremy's vehicle got hit with a depleted uranium rocket, he thrust himself headlong out of his vehicle. After checking on the Husky driver, who was unhurt, he scrambled to Jeremy's vehicle to render aid to those wounded. All four of their comrades sustained injuries, three of them seriously. Fortunately, the ambush wasn't a complex attack where the enemy came at them from multiple sides. Since all the vehicles turned and faced the enemy, the National Guard unit had no fire power facing the other direction. In the chaos and confusion, they quickly ran out of ammo. Nick and the others from his unit grabbed more rounds and fed them to the gunners, coaching them to get positive identification of the enemy (PID) and then to shoot with controlled bursts watching their rate of fire rather than spraying bullets haphazardly in the direction of the combatants.

The MRAP that Jeremy rode in took three depleted uranium 80 mm rounds, which moved the thirty-thousand-pound vehicle across the road and into a ditch. The first round decimated the AC unit dispersing Freon throughout the interior of the vehicle. One of the soldiers inhaled a large amount of it resulting in severe lung damage. The second rocket hit high and toward the front activating the halon fire-suppression gas. The third one pierced the armored vehicle across from where Jeremy sat, completely severing the lower leg of that soldier. It also shredded the shin and calf of Jeremy's leg. Despite their own wounds, Jeremy and his comrades ensured that the wounded National Guard soldiers in their vehicle had put on tourniquets properly. As the interior compartment filled with halon and Freon, the rear ramp wouldn't respond to the driver's controls.

One of Jeremy's comrades, despite a severe wound, quickly hit the ramp button located in the rear of the vehicle to allow the fumes and the soldiers to exit, preventing everyone from suffocating. Jeremy ensured that everyone else got out first. When the convoy called for close air support from the A-10 Thunderbolts, the enemy had maneuvered so close to the convoy that the U.S. soldiers heard the impact of the 30 mm rounds from the Avenger rotary cannon. The firefight lasted about forty-five minutes by the time that the A-10s neutralized the enemy. While pulling Big Country out of the MRAP, Nick jammed his neck due to Jeremy's size. He, along with other uninjured soldiers, tended to the wounded now outside lying on the ground, tightening everyone's tourniquets. With the enemy eradicated, they called for the medevacs.

While the convoy arranged for wrecker crews to salvage the disabled vehicles and for another unit to deal with unexploded ordnance, the medics stabilized the wounded. Nick remembered seeing a tibia bone lying on the floor of the MRAP. The soldier to whom it belonged later woke up in a hospital in Germany with his leg amputated above the knee. Nick, assisted by Afghan soldiers, ended up carrying Big Country to the medevac choppers just like he did so many times in training back at Fort Campbell. In all, six soldiers including Jeremy were air lifted while the rest of the wounded rode back to their home FOB by vehicles. The Army then transported Jeremy and a few of his comrades to Walter Reed National Military Medical Center for long term treatment.

Almost three months later, on September 21, 2010, while assigned to a COP located about two and a half klicks from an FOB, Nick and his comrades received orders to patrol and locate a suspected mortar site. A Taliban mortar team had fired upon the FOB on a consistent basis. Two squads of infantry, a team of engineers, and a platoon of Afghan soldiers comprised the detail. As the patrol came down off a roof into an alleyway, Nick assisted each soldier to the ground. After all the American soldiers had gone by, Nick then assisted the first two Afghans down off the roof and into the alley. As he turned to help the next soldier, the first two Afghans stepped on the pressure plate of an IED. The explosion disintegrated the two Afghans and peppered Nick from behind with shrapnel.

Allied forces found it difficult to detect pressure plates because the Taliban used plastic and wood, which couldn't be picked up by metal detectors. Once emplaced, the rain would harden the dirt over them and sometimes even moved the pressure plates a bit. Often times the enemy emplaced an inactive IED and later paid somebody to hook the explosive to the battery. Soldiers rolled the dice every time they left the wire. If one constantly worried about where one stepped, then that person didn't move far. If luck smiled on a soldier when stepping on a pressure plate, only the blasting cap would explode and not the main charge. IEDs could be made out of anything such as a coke can or candle holders. As combat engineers, they had to get good at terrain detection and change detection (noticing things out of place).

As a result of the explosion, Nick went through sixteen months of rehabilitation. While on convalescent leave in November, Nick, along with his wife Abby and his father-in-law, visited Jeremy at Walter Reed. Nine years later, Nick still had shrapnel working its way out of his body, causing irritation, bruises, and pits in his skin. He received a PTSD diagnosis of general anxiety disorder. He used to have bad nightmares regularly but now just every few months. At the high point of suffering horrific dreams, Nick screamed and thrashed in bed in the middle of the night, while Abby apprehensively stood in the dark corner of the room desperately pondering how she could ease her husband's torment. Even today, Nick moved as far over on the road as possible when passing cars as an instinctive cautionary measure. Over time, his hardened emotions softened up and began to function like they used to, for he had the ability to handle trauma better than most of his comrades. No matter how bad his day unfolded, he assured himself that life would be better tomorrow.

Throughout his time in the Army, Nick encountered a myriad of soldiers who knew Jeremy. The extent of Big Country's brotherhood and friendship with fellow soldiers reached far and wide. Jeremy was the kindest, most considerate person you would ever meet while also being one of the most ferocious warriors. A dichotomy difficult to comprehend. Nick didn't understand why good people like Jeremy struggled and suffered so much with PTSD. Regardless, Jeremy would always loom large in Nick's heart, a legacy no one or nothing could take away. When Nick went through chemotherapy, Jeremy spent hours, sometimes all night, at the hospital talking with him or playing the guitar for him. At such times, every nurse on the ward gravitated into the room to hear Big Country play.

Jeremy always focused on others, never himself. As the years went by, he spent hours at Nick's house in the summer teaching Nick's nephew how to play the guitar better, meticulously showing him how to hold each finger for each cord until he got it right. Big Country always went out of his way to do things for others. He dropped everything to help someone in need and gave the shirt off his back never asking for anything in return. When Jeremy went through a tough time himself, he never asked for assistance but kept his focus always on others. Whenever Nick had a problem, he called Jeremy who always made time for him and turned a gloomy scenario into a positive outlook. He had a great sense of humor and did great voice impersonations to make anyone laugh and feel better about life no matter what the situation.

Slowly, however, Jeremy became paranoid, convinced that someone out there constantly watched him and wanted to kill him. He didn't feel safe unless he carried a weapon with him all the time. Nick tried to reassure Big Country that no one pursued him, but Jeremy wouldn't believe it. After selling his house and moving back with his parents, he showed notable recovery, becoming the Jeremy that everyone knew beforehand. Nick often wondered if he did enough to help his friend. He knew, though, of Big Country's stubborn streak and his propensity to do what he set his mind on regardless if Nick advised otherwise. Despite Nick's urging, Jeremy never seriously sought help for emotional and mental issues. Mental health challenges carried such a stigma in the military, that many soldiers kept their problems to themselves. Even if a military buddy reached out to help, most soldiers denied that they had a problem. Jeremy's Iraq experience haunted him most, partly because some of his icons died while he survived. On one occasion, the unit 1SG pulled Jeremy from a convoy and took his place much to Jeremy's chagrin. That patrol got hit hard resulting in many casualties. Subsequently, Jeremy suffered from survivor's guilt. Nick wished that he could have had some way to help his dear friend through all that.

8

A Good Shepherd

Terry and Jill asked Pastor Herb Mays to attend the gathering of family
and friends who assembled that day on behalf of Jeremy. He and Jeremy had
a close friendship. Pastor Herb was a Vietnam War veteran who wrestled
with PTSD for over forty years. Because he and Jeremy had a lot in common, Jeremy enjoyed talking with Pastor Herb and could relate to him. He
had tremendous respect and admiration for the pastor. Some days earlier,
Jeremy called Pastor Herb to talk. Jeremy found it difficult to believe that
God could love and forgive him for the things that he did in combat. He
became a highly efficient, ferocious warrior resulting in the death of many.
He loved performing his duty in combat to the highest degree. The military leadership called on him to perform those combat tasks that resulted
in much carnage because they knew he would do it well. His devotion to
duty and propensity to follow orders without question compelled him to be
so. They often called upon him in order to spare the younger soldiers the
trauma of such missions. He, himself, often selflessly volunteered to take the
place of other soldiers so that they could remain back at base. Years later,
though, he felt permanently condemned for the carnage that he participated
in, confessing to others that he became a monster that loved to kill. Unable
to forgive himself, he couldn't believe that God would forgive him.

Pastor Herb first met Jeremy there at the church around January 2004.
His sister, Leah, sang on the worship team. Home on leave after finishing basic training, he came to Sunday service in uniform, a sharp-looking young
man. Pastor talked to him a bit after church. Jeremy only came a few times
before he had to go to his duty station. Pastor then lost contact with him
after that. In 2013, Terry and Jill asked Pastor Herb to go to Jeremy's house
in Dawson Springs, Kentucky to encourage him because he was having a

rough time with life. Upon doing so, Pastor immediately saw that he had major emotional problems. When Pastor arrived, he noticed that Jeremy had black paper covering all the windows of his house. Pastor spoke with Jeremy and prayed over his home. He continually encouraged Jeremy to go to the VA hospital in Nashville to speak with the doctors there who helped him so much in dealing with his PTSD from the Vietnam War. For whatever reason, Jeremy never went. It seemed that he had animus toward the VA and wouldn't go even though he needed a lot of help.

In 2015, Jeremy started attending The River at Portland Church on a regular basis and later played guitar on the worship team, after some of the musicians strongly encouraged him to join. Once he became a regular attendee at the church, he came in early on Sunday mornings and talked with Pastor, who usually allocated the time before church to pray alone in his office. However, he gladly made time for Jeremy if he wanted to talk. After several conversations, Pastor discerned that the incident where Jeremy fired upon a vehicle that ran a roadblock really tormented him because a little girl got killed. Jeremy never conquered that demon. Pastor begged him to go see the two doctors that personally helped him deal with his combat related anxiety. But Jeremy never did, perhaps because he didn't want to relive his combat experience and confront the things that haunted him. He just wanted to get it all out of his mind. Unfortunately, a warrior never forgot combat completely. At seventy-four years old, Pastor sometimes saw or heard things that triggered a torrent of combat memories flooding into his mind. Since it never left him, he learned, over a period of time, to take charge of and manage it, so that it no longer controlled or rendered him helpless.

In Pastor Herb's eyes, Jeremy had a bigger-than-life persona with an outgoing personality. Physically, he was a mountain of a man. Underneath all that lived a gentle little boy who never met a stranger and always focused on other people rather than himself. The other members of the worship team absolutely loved him. When he came into Pastor's office, he meekly asked him about his experiences in Vietnam. Jeremy had a historical interest in the Vietnam War, the missions that they did, how they survived, and such. Pastor told him that they fought in the jungle to defeat the enemy and survive as best they could. Jeremy eagerly soaked up all the information about that war that Pastor gave him. The two veterans had some good talks in that office. Despite his daily suffering from serving in combat and animus toward the system afterward, Jeremy, completely pro-Army, never once badmouthed his military service. He never regretted fighting the war on terror. In Pastor Herb's office, Jeremy seemed upbeat and outgoing. He found it a safe and trusted place. Pastor recognized the young man's solid patriotism despite the immense emotional turmoil. He deeply loved this country, the Army, and the United States flag.

One Sunday, Jeremy had a great experience with God when holy power overwhelmed this behemoth of a man and filled him with perfect peace. There he knelt at the foot of the altar praising God. Watching this unfold encouraged Pastor Herb that Jeremy would make progress. Jeremy called Pastor the next day, his voice exuberant with joy and vitality. He seemed on top of the world. Then on that Friday morning, Jill called Pastor Herb and told him of Jeremy's daunting disposition. With all joy gone, emotionally defeated in disbelief, and bearing a broken heart for Jeremy, Pastor almost decided to leave the ministry agonizing within, *What's the use?*

Three days later, during the gathering to honor Jeremy Doyle Smith, Pastor Herb rose at the appointed time, walked to the front of the room, and, with a wavering voice, addressed the gathering as follows:

> I'm honored to do the homegoing of my buddy. Jeremy and I were close. I was not only his pastor, but I was a friend of his. You had to love the guy. Jeremy was really a funny guy. He would arrive early to church sometimes, come into my office, and ask, "Pastor, you're an old Vietnam vet. How did you all do it over there?"
>
> I said, "We did it the same way over there as you guys do it over here. We tried to survive and have another day."
>
> He was interested in what we did in Vietnam all these years ago. He called me Monday. And it is just a shock to be here today, one week later, to do his homegoing. And really, a funeral is for dead people. This is a homegoing. Jeremy is alive. He's more alive today than he has ever been. But he called me Monday, and we talked a long time. He was so excited about Sunday morning service. When I answered the phone, he said, "Pastor, I got something I want to ask you."
>
> And at our church, you come into the driveway, and we got flags, the United States flags on one side and Israeli are on the other side. You come into the driveway of our church on the hill and there are all these flags. Well, about three weeks ago, the rope for one of the United States flags broke. I went out, got the flag, and brought it in. I can't shimmy the pole, so I secured the flag until I could get it put back up. Not a soul in our church has said one thing about that flag missing in the middle of this driveway. Jeremy noticed that flag, and so he called me Monday morning, and the first thing he said was, "Now Pastor, I'm going to tell you something." He said, "For the last three weeks, I have come in here, and you got a flag missing."

I said, "I know. I'm wanting to get it up. The rope broke, and I got nobody to put it back up."

He said, "I'm going to tell you something. Sunday morning, if that flag is not hung, I'm coming in, getting that flag, and shimmying up that pole to put that flag back up."

I said, "Jeremy, look brother, you're three hundred fifty pounds! And you're going to shimmy up that pole and put the flag back up? I don't think so!" But I knew he was serious enough about that flag that I got a guy at the church named Bob. I said, "Now Bob, we got a problem here. I got a guy that's about three hundred fifty pounds who's upset about this flag. So, we're going to put this flag up." So, I told Bob, "Go get me a ladder." So, he's climbing the ladder, and I said, "Wrap your hand around the pole. In case the ladder falls, just shimmy down the pole."

Well, he's shaking like a leaf in the wind and asked me, "Is it okay?"

I said, "Don't worry. If it's not okay and you fall, we'll pray and believe that God will raise you up and everything will be alright."

Jeremy, the flag is up. Believe me.

You know, I see all these guys here that served with Jeremy. If you're here today and served in the military with him, I want you to stand. God bless you! We honor you and thank you.

Jill told me that Jeremy had a favorite scripture in the Bible, so I'm going to minister on that a little bit. In the Bible in the eleventh chapter of John we see the story where Lazarus has died. And so, the sisters come to Jesus, and starting with the nineteenth verse, we read these words, "And many of the Jews had come to Martha and Mary, to console them about their brother. So, then Martha, when she heard that Jesus was coming, went to meet Him, but Mary stayed in the house. Martha then said to Jesus, 'Lord, if You had been here, my brother would not have died. Even now I know that whatever You ask of God, God will give You.'" This passage goes on to say, "Jesus said to her, 'Your brother will rise *from the dead.*' Martha said to Him, 'I know that he will rise in the resurrection on the last day.' Jesus said to her, 'I am the resurrection and the life; the one who believes in Me will live, even if he dies, and everyone who lives and believes in Me will never die. Do you believe this?'"

Jeremy Smith is not dead. This is his shell, but he's not dead. He's more alive today than he has ever been.

Then Jesus goes to see Mary. "So when Mary came *to the place* where Jesus was, she saw Him and fell at His feet, saying to Him, 'Lord, if You had been here, my brother would not have died.' Therefore when Jesus saw her weeping, and the Jews who came with her *also* weeping, He was deeply moved in spirit and was troubled, and He said, 'Where have you laid him?' They said to Him, 'Lord, come and see.'" Verse thirty-five says that Jesus wept. Jesus did not weep because Lazarus was dead. Jesus wept because of their unbelief. The blind-eye healer walked right beside her. The demon-deliverer was walking with her. But they couldn't believe. When they got in their biggest trials and troubles, and Jesus was walking with them, they still couldn't believe. And Jesus wept over their unbelief, because He knew that He was going to raise Lazarus up. Now, they go over, and Jesus said, "Where's the tomb?"

So, they take Jesus to the tomb. And so, everybody around Jesus is saying, "Now, Lord, are You sure? He has been dead for four days. He doesn't smell good."

The Bible says that he stinketh four days. In response, Jesus said this. He had to call Lazarus by name, because if He hadn't, all of them would have come out of the tombs. But He went and He said, "Lazarus, come forth!" And he rose from the dead. And Jesus said, "Loose him and let him go."

Thursday of this past week, Jeremy Smith was loosed. Jesus Christ of Nazareth loosed him of all of his trials, of all of his sorrows, of all of his disappointments, of all of his hurt in his body. Do you understand that Jeremy Smith is not wounded today? He's a whole man. He does not have part of his leg missing. He is complete, a new creation in Jesus Christ. And he's more alive than we can ever imagine today, but he's loose from all of that torment and all of this brokenness in his body. I talked to Jeremy lots of times. And Jeremy told me, "Pastor, I just can't understand how Jesus could love me. How could He love me?"

I said, "Jeremy, He loves you because He gave His life for you."

But Jeremy said, "But you don't understand what I've done!"

I said, "It doesn't matter what you've done. The Bible says that if any man is in Christ, he's a new creation, and old things are passed away." I said, "Do you understand, Jeremy, that everything has been washed away. When you accept Jesus as your savior, it's as if there is no sin in your life." And I know where Jeremy is. I have had talks with him, and I know that he was saved and is in heaven.

In Second Corinthians, we see an interesting passage of scripture that Paul wrote. He said in 2 Cor 5:1, "For we know that if our earthly tent which is our house." Paul called the body a tent, so he knew it would be temporary. We're only going to be here a short period of time, some longer than others, some shorter. This body is temporary. It's going to disintegrate and be nothing. But the real man that Jesus created in us is our spirit-man. And Paul said this, "We have a building from God, a house not made by hands, eternal in the heavens. For indeed, in this *tent* we groan, longing to be clothed with our dwelling from heaven." Then he said in verse four, "For indeed, we who are in this tent groan, being burdened, because we do not want to be unclothed but to be clothed, so that what is mortal will be swallowed up by life. Now He who prepared us for this very *purpose is* God, who gave us the Spirit as a pledge." So, when we accept Jesus Christ as our savior, it is a guarantee that we're going to have that place prepared for us. "Therefore, being always of good courage, and knowing that while we are at home in the body we are absent from the Lord—for we walk by faith, not by sight—but we are of good courage and prefer rather to be absent from the body and to be at home with the Lord."

The word of God is true. When Jeremy took his last breath on this earth, the next breath he took was in heaven. And he's alive today. Jill, you and Terry will see your little boy again. And you know what? You're not going to see your little boy hurting. You're not going to see your little boy broken. You're going to see your little boy whole. You're going to see your little boy as you sent him off to war. And we thank God for that because Jesus has promised that to us.

In John the fourteenth chapter, we're talking about what he has given us. In the fourteenth chapter of John, we see what he's done for us. He said, "Do not let your heart be troubled; believe in God, believe also in Me. In My Father's house are many rooms; if *that* were not so, I would have told you." This is Jesus talking, "And if I go and prepare a place for you, I am coming again and will take you to Myself, so that where I am, *there* you also will be. And you know the way where I am going.' Thomas said to Him, 'Lord, we do not know where You are going; how do we know the way?' Jesus said to him, 'I am the way, and the truth, and the life; no one comes to the Father except through Me.'" The only way to be in heaven clothed in the habitation of God is to know Jesus Christ as your personal savior.

Now, we know that he prepared that for us. And sometimes, it's interesting to find out what's not there in order to find out what's really there, somewhere. Now we know, that in heaven, we are a spirit-man with a new created body. This is just my opinion, that I want to be about six foot two, 185 pounds, and look like Arnold Schwarzenegger. I want that as my heavenly body. That's what I'd like to have. But you know, I'm going to leave it up to Jesus, and I know that it's going to be good. But, what's not there, number one, there's no doctors in heaven. You ain't going to need no doctors because there's no sickness in heaven. So, the doctors are out of business in heaven. You know what's going to happen? You're going to go to heaven one day, and you're going to see your doctor that probably did your appendix or took out your gall bladder. And you're going to say, "Buster, I remember you. But the one thing I remember about you is that you overcharged me!" And you're going to say, "Well, I'm going to forgive you anyway." You got to forgive him. He's in heaven, right? You can't hold a grudge in heaven. So, there's no doctors. There're no hospitals.

There're no police officers in heaven; not going to need none of that. No bankers to charge you 28 percent interest on your money because you're going to have everything you need up there. You ain't gonna have to buy nothing. It's all free. Everything's good. And God's got the ultimate fast food. You know, you're in heaven and you say, "Well, I think I want a coke today." Zip! He prepared that for us so we could have that.

I'm excited to tell you about Jesus, and that Jeremy, right here, he's with Jesus. He's not in this body. He's with Jesus. Now, I will tell you what else there isn't. There're no more tears in heaven. There's no more crying in heaven. Rev 21:4 says that God will wipe all your tears. You'll have no more sorrow. There will be no more bad Mondays. Those days are gone. There will be no more bad days. Can you imagine living in the bliss of heaven and never have a bad day? Never have Monday morning blues. Everything's going to be okay. So, there's no pain because the Bible says that the old things are passed away.

When Jill called me Friday, hurting, and gave me the news, she asked me if her little boy was okay. I said, "Your little boy is more alive today, than he's ever been. He's walking the streets of glory." And I'll tell you what, the Bible talks in the fourteenth chapter of John about mansions. There's going to be beautiful places. You know, a lot of preachers don't preach on this because a lot of them don't believe it. I believe every word from Genesis to Revelation. I believe that God's got a place for me. I believe he's made that place for us. And if we accept Jesus Christ as Savior then it's for us. But he said that there's many mansions.

I can imagine Thursday when Jeremy walked into the portals of glory. There's got to be an escort to show him what all he had. Knowing Jeremy, I can imagine that this is what he said. He goes into heaven and the escort takes him by the hand and says,

"Jeremy, I want to show you the promised land and what God prepared for you."

And I just imagine that probably Jeremy's mansion is on a little hill. Jesus had to have decorated it in green and army colors and all that. It probably has the infantry logo up on the door. And after looking at that mansion, I imagine that this is what Jeremy said. "My God, what a bunker! This is something else."

But what's there in heaven is love, joy, and tranquility from the peace of God, which is forever. No one's mad at anyone in heaven. They're all happy, a wonderful river of life there, the throne of God. You know what you do in heaven? You worship God. There's no night there, and we worship God for eternity. You know, you don't have birthdays in heaven. It's not like you live there for two thousand years, and someone asks, "How old are you today?" You don't know because there's no birthdays. You stay the same as you are. Terry and Jill, you're going to see your little boy just like he was. And we see that God has prepared all this for us, those that love Him.

I talked to Jeremy, and he knew the Lord even though he was troubled. And he went through a lot. And we anguished with him. He would tell me things that happened. And sometimes I just didn't know what to say. But I know that he's not suffering today. I know that. He called me last Monday morning and we talked a long time. He said, "Pastor, I want to tell you what happened on Sunday." He was playing guitar up on the stage. He was in the praise and worship team at our church, and they all loved him. He was just like a big bear. Everyone gravitates toward him. He said, "On Sunday, as we were praising God, I walked off the stage and over to you. I said all my life that I would never bow to any man." Jeremy's big enough that he could back that up. He said, "But Sunday morning I walked over to where you were at the edge of the stage. I reached out to touch you, and the power of God came in through the top of my head and knocked me to the floor on my knees. It was the most peaceful feeling."

I look back now, and I see that God was preparing Jeremy for heaven on Sunday morning. There's no doubt in my mind because he knows all things. And Jeremy told me, "Pastor, it was the most wonderful feeling in my life. I never felt such peace in my life. When the power of God came, it went all the way through my body to my feet. For an hour, I couldn't drive or do anything. I was just under the presence of God." You see, that's what we are going to have in heaven, all that. And Jeremy said, "Do you know that the old marine who's in the church came up to me afterward and said that everything was going to be alright?" God was dealing with Jeremy Sunday. God prepared Jeremy for heaven Sunday morning. I want you to know today that in our natural bodies here, we grieve. I've heard people say that time heals all wounds. No, it doesn't. Time gives you the ability to cope. It doesn't heal that wound, but it will give you the ability to cope. It's only through the precious Holy Spirit that you and your family get through this.

The last words that Jeremy spoke to me on the phone were, "Pastor, I want to tell you one thing. I want you to know that I love you." He always told me that he loved me, and he would always hug me. It's like getting a hug from superman. He'd squeeze me like a big bear. I would think, *Oh my God! I'm an old man.* He further said, "I hope I live long enough to be exactly like you."

I said, "Jeremy, you're like me now. Do you understand that we're blood brothers? We share DNA from serving and fighting on foreign soil. I understand that we are blood brothers."

Jesus spoke one time saying, "If I were thirsty, would you give me a drink? If I were hungry, would you give me something to eat? If I needed your coat, would you give me your coat?" Jeremy, buddy, I give you my coat.

As tears streamed down his face, Pastor Herb took off his suit coat and draped it over Jeremy's chest in the casket. They shared a common thread as combat veterans. Jeremy loved and trusted Pastor Herb to watch his back. Now, the coat off the back of his dear friend and battle buddy would comfort Jeremy for eternity. Then Pastor Herb concluded:

Let's pray. Father, I thank you and praise you, today, that you have given me the ability to do this when it seemed impossible, Lord. By your grace and your mercy, you enabled me to hopefully impart something positive to the people today. Lord, I ask you by the precious Holy Spirit to minister to the family and friends and loved ones here, that we remember the good times with Jeremy, remember all the laughs and hugs, and all the things that were so wonderful that he did for us. I thank you, Lord.

I'm going to ask you here at this funeral home. You may be here and may not know Jesus as your savior. I challenge you, that if you never accepted Jesus as your savior, that you need to do that. Heaven is real, and hell is real. But heaven is for the saved. I would ask you to pray about that. God bless you.

9

Jeremy's Final Chapter

WHILE JEREMY FOUGHT IN war, Jill asked God for tangible reassurance of her son's safety, similar to the gesture that Gideon made in Judges, chapter 6. Gideon humbly requested a sign to confirm God's commission upon him. Jill knew that the Lord watched over Jeremy but still wanted a sign for reassurance. She asked God to send her son butterflies during his deployment either in dreams or physically, so many that he would comment to her about the multitude that he encountered. Subsequently, she anxiously awaited during each phone call for him to speak of butterflies. Jeremy never did. Jill even asked him once what he thought of the bugs and butterflies over there. He replied, "Well, Mom, they're like the ones at home, only the spiders are bigger."

Her request unfulfilled, Jill felt dejected. Then that dreadful day occurred in July 2010—Jeremy got severely wounded. While waiting for flight tickets to Walter Reed National Military Medical Center, Jill started painting porch furniture to occupy herself and keep her mind from fretting over her injured son. With the porch swing resting upon sawhorses, she painted away as butterflies started descending around her. They landed all over the breezeway, landed on the wet paint, and landed on her shoulder and hands. At first, Jill shooed them away in irritation. Then she stopped and looked about in amazement to see butterflies swarming everywhere, encompassing the porch area of her little country home. She had never seen so many butterflies at one time in all her life. As she gasped at the marvelous sight, God's still voice spoke to her spirit saying, "I AM. I am with Jeremy, and I am also with you."

Irritation turned to elation as Jill knew that God had answered her request. She shared the experience with Jeremy, who listened with astonishment. That entire summer, butterflies flourished abundantly in the county and at the Smith house which sat upon a quiet country lane. Even other people in the community commented on how they had never seen so many butterflies before in their lives. Jill simply smiled at their comments. From then on, butterflies became a connection between Jeremy and her.

During the beginning of 2017, Jeremy finally sold his house and moved back in with his parents. Over the next year and a half, he began to do better and even quit drinking in May 2018. He shook his fist and resolutely declared, "God give me the strength. I never want to drink again!" Shortly thereafter, he began to exhibit unusual symptoms. He experienced blood in his urine, vomiting, and diarrhea. He fretted over the prospect that he acquired radiation poisoning from the depleted uranium shrapnel in his leg. Consequently, he scheduled himself for a test to determine low dose radiation effects on soldiers with depleted uranium in their bodies. Jeremy had to remain clean and sober for the test. For thirty days, he abstained from all drugs and alcohol that he had used in the past to manage the pain. The nerve damage pain in his wounded leg became excruciating and unbearable. Mental anguish compounded this physical torment because Jeremy dreaded the possibility that he had radiation poisoning. This prospect tortured him. He felt helplessly trapped in a pit of doom from which he could not escape.

A few weeks before the test, he began to drink alcohol again. Tears rolling down his face, he apologized to Terry for taking up the bottle again. Terry stated that he owed no apology to anyone. He understood Jeremy's predicament and probably would do the same thing himself. That Sunday, Jeremy had an incredible encounter with God at the foot of the altar during the church service. He spoke with Pastor Herb on the phone the next day exuberant about life. As Monday and Tuesday waned on, however, the darkness tenaciously and methodically crept back into his psyche. Thoughts of radiation sickness hounded him as dark voices tauntingly insisted that his life would never get better.

That Wednesday, Jill came home from work to have lunch with Jeremy as she did every day. Pulling into the driveway, she noticed him standing there with an odd, startled expression on his face. He looked worried, even somewhat shocked. Nervous, Jill pulled up beside him and queried, "Hi, Son. Are you okay?"

He replied, "Mom, when I came out earlier to go to the store, butterflies were all over my truck." He continued emphatically, "Mom, you don't understand. I mean it. Butterflies covered my entire truck. What do you think?"

With the comforting assurance that only a mom could provide, Jill said, "Jeremy, it's nothing to worry about. It's just the Lord reassuring you that he is with you. It's a good thing." However, the incident startled her as well. She thought, *What a sight to behold, but what did it mean?* She had no idea of what the next day held in store for the Smith family.

After they enjoyed lunch together, Jeremy gave his mom a hearty bear hug and just wouldn't let go. He said over and over how much he loved her. Jill discerned that something unusual was happening. She said, "I know you're upset about a lot of things, but there's something else going on. What's wrong?"

Jeremy simply sat back down in his chair at the lunch table, slumped his shoulders, and said nothing. As Jill began to leave to go back to work, he again hugged her profusely. Later that evening, as Terry wearily prepared to go to bed, Jeremy beseeched him to stay up and spend time with him.

When Jill came home on Thursday to have lunch with her son, she found the kitchen disheveled with wall décor and spilled milk on the floor. All his life, Jeremy diligently cleaned up any mess that he made in the house. As her heart sank to her feet, she concluded that something just wasn't right. She found Jeremy in a deep sleep on the couch with a dirty plate on the carpet. Wishing to wake him up for lunch but not wanting to startle him, she made as much noise banging cabinet doors and heavily placing items on the counter as she could, hoping the commotion would rouse him. Nothing worked. She ate lunch alone that day. Later that afternoon, Terry arrived home from work to find Jeremy asleep in his room. On her way home from work, Jill stopped and got chicken with macaroni and cheese, one of Jeremy's favorite meals. When Jeremy came out of his room, she gleefully announced, "Hey Jeremy, on the way home, I picked up one of your favorites for dinner."

He replied, "I'll catch that later, Mom." He then gave Jill a hearty hug. As she looked up at him, she could tell that he used every bit of strength within him not to cry. He then uttered, "I love you, Mom." Turning to Terry, Jeremy hugged his dad emphatically as well and said, "See you later. I'm going out."

Terry replied with subdued confusion, "See you later, Son."

As Jeremy walked out the door, every fiber of Jill's being cried out, "Go after him! Go after him! Go after him!" Rationale prevailed, and she restrained herself from doing so. Even if she had submitted to her intuition, Jeremy would have just grimaced at her for treating him like a child. This thirty-four-year-old, six-foot-two combat veteran, weighing three hundred fifty pounds, came and went as he pleased. He usually returned before his parents went to bed so he could bid them good night. However, on Thursday night, August 2, 2018, that didn't occur, another out-of-the-norm event during that week.

Jeremy had gone to a friend's house to self-medicate with alcohol. His friends noticed that he was angrier and more upset than usual. He shared with them his fear of having radiation poisoning and told them of his symptoms. He informed them that he dreaded going for the test on Monday and the resulting prognosis. Would they amputate his leg or give him a death sentence? His friends tried to encourage him by pointing out that he hadn't even taken the test yet to know the results. Thus, there was no use being so negative. The physical and emotional pain he encountered that past month crescendoed into an extreme drinking binge that night, as he consumed a tremendous amount of alcohol in a short period of time. Drowsy and confused, Jeremy got loud and obnoxious. His friends coaxed him into a bedroom and laid him on the floor with a pillow and blanket.

While he lay there in the dark, the dangerously high alcohol content prevented his body from metabolizing the liquor out of his bloodstream. As a result, the alcohol content kept increasing as more of it seeped from his stomach and intestines into his circulation. Alone and engulfed by gloom, he wrestled once again with his torments. He felt like he lay upon a spinning top. Round-and-round was the last sensation he mindfully noted before passing out. Because of the catastrophic concentration of alcohol that accumulated in his system, his brain no longer properly controlled vital functions performed by his heart and lungs. His breathing and heartbeat slowed causing his body temperature to drop.

Sometime during this juncture, with his body and soul swallowed up by dense shadow, Jeremy stopped breathing, his heart stopped beating, and his eternal spirit departed for the everlasting light never to hearken the darkness again. Terry's pride and joy, Jill's little baby bunting boy, and Leah's awesome big brother died while lying alone in the eclipse of a solitary room. His friends checked in on him, found him unresponsive with a blue complexion, and called 9-1-1. The emergency medical technicians arrived but couldn't revive him. He was gone. The little boy outraged by the plight of hungry children, the young man who gave his hard-earned money to help others, the selfless soldier who volunteered for more than his fair share of combat missions to spare his brothers, the patriot who defended freedom and liberty by fighting in the war on terror had perished.

Later that night, the police attempted to contact Terry and Jill by phone. However, neither of them slept with their phones nearby. The police then dispatched a cruiser to their house and knocked on the front door to no avail, so they left a note on the garage door requesting that the Smiths contact them. On August 2, 2018, Leah's phone lit up at midnight. She peered blearily about at the shadows of her darkened room, gaining cognizance. Looking groggily toward her phone, she assumed that she received a marketing email from a retailer, rolled back over, and beckoned the deep sleep she had been enjoying. Awakened by her crying child a couple hours later, Leah checked her phone to see a missed call from Franklin, Kentucky. She texted Jeremy asking him if he was okay. Receiving no response, she called her brother only to be greeted by the cold dejection of continual ringing. Worry began to flail about in the heart of the young woman. She googled the number of the missed call, which came back as belonging to the Simpson County Sheriff Department. Her first thought was that Jeremy had ended up in jail again for some reason. Panic set in as she frantically tried to gather her thoughts. Since this would be his third arrest, he would probably stay in jail for a good while. She called the number only to get no response. She then called the Franklin Police Department but ended up speaking to the Bowling Green Police instead. She explained the situation to which they replied that someone would get back with her.

The next five minutes felt like an eternity as Leah sat in the murky mist of the wee hours of morning staring at her phone. Anxiety and concern swirled all over her. As her phone rang, she stared in horror at it momentarily. With a trembling hand, she picked up her phone, hurried to the bathroom, and answered the call. A police official asked if she was in Franklin, Kentucky where they could talk to her in person. She explained that she lived near Nashville, Tennessee. The official kept repeating that they really needed to speak with her in person. Finally, Leah insisted that it was three in the morning, and she was sixty miles away. Dumbfounded, she started to think that somehow, she was in trouble with the law. Finally, the official stated that Jeremy died that night. Everything went black as Leah desperately grabbed at the wall to keep from falling to her knees. He apologized for informing her over the phone and that they tried unsuccessfully to contact her parents. They were only able to leave a note for them on their garage door. He briefly explained what had occurred with her brother that fateful night and gave her the phone number of the responding officer who arrived at the scene.

The harsh reality that her parents didn't yet know suddenly consumed her. She began to weep. Her husband entered the room and asked what was wrong. She put her hand on his chest, looked into his eyes, and behind streaming tears stated, "Jeremy died." Resolutely, Leah declared to her husband that she had to leave immediately for Franklin to tell her parents. She walked into her bedroom and wandered in circles a few times as a myriad of thoughts raced through her mind. Finally, she managed to dress and left for Kentucky. The drive to her parents' house seemed the darkest, longest trek of her life. At first, shock subdued any other emotion. As she got on the interstate, deep dread barged its way into her heart as she began to weep and then cry hysterically. Plunged into deep despair, she pulled over and called her best friend to no avail. There she sat in the darkest of predawn hours, alone in her car on the side of the road crying profusely, a dismal solitary figure consumed by shadow. After a short while, she called the phone number of the officer who had responded to the scene. He gave her more details as to what happened to her brother that night.

With those details in mind, Leah forged onward toward her parents' house planning her strategy of how best to notify them of the terrible turmoil and tragedy now looming over the Smith family. First, she would lure them gently to the kitchen where she would give them each a cup of coffee to calm them. Then she would gingerly tell them the tragic news. As her mind bantered around these thoughts, an inexplicable calm overcame her as she pulled into the driveway of her parents' home. No time for hysterics. She had to remain calm and tend to the important task at hand. She got out of her car at 4:10 that morning and walked passed the hallowed ground where Jeremy dropped to kiss the soil of America when he returned home from war. She grabbed the police note off the garage door and walked past the porch post upon which tattered Old Glory perched those many months as they prayed for Jeremy's safe return from combat. She entered the dim, quiet house. As she passed Jeremy's room, she resisted the flood of emotions that tried to trespass upon her soul. Entering her parents' room, she called out to her mom several times.

Somewhat awakened yet perplexed, Jill insisted several times, "Leah, what's wrong? Why are you here?" At this juncture, Leah realized that her carefully laid out plans to gently inform her parents of their son's demise were futile. Looking into the dark room and talking to two faceless people, Leah asked her dad if he was awake. After hearing him move and grumble a bit, she told them the tragic news. She simply said, "Jeremy died." Jill became frantic. As her parents got out of bed, Leah walked to the kitchen and sat down emotionally exhausted. After getting dressed and trying to gain composure, Jill went to the kitchen, began to make coffee, stared Leah straight in the eyes, and demanded incredulously, "Are you telling me that my son is dead?" Regardless of how hard she tried, Leah couldn't utter her answer. She just couldn't say those words again. She simply nodded in the affirmative.

At this point, Terry entered the kitchen, looked at Jill, and then looked at Leah. As he bent over to hug his daughter, he broke into uncontrollable weeping for the only time in his life. He wept deeply for the loss of his son. He wept deeply for the suffering Jeremy endured to defend freedom. He wept deeply for the suffering that his dad, Leo, endured to preserve liberty. All the anguish Terry suffered over the past fifty years for the sake of these blessings manifested emotionally at that moment in a torrential flood of tears. Shocked to see her dad in this disposition, all Leah could think to do was to wrap her arms around him and gently rub his back.

After Terry regained his composure, Leah answered a few of their questions and gave her parents the phone number to the police officer who responded to the scene of their son's demise. Engulfed in this surreal morning, Terry and Jill called the officer to gather more information. All day long, it felt as if the air around them had completely evaporated. Breathing seemed impossible. All that day, the Smith family labored at the emotionally arduous task of calling relatives and friends to inform them of Jeremy's passing. As they informed each person via phone call, they struggled to keep composure as the person on the other end of the line broke down in tears. Upon concluding the phone call, the Smith family too broke out weeping. Thus, they repeated this ominous ritual countless times that terrible day.

As Kelly Pierce lay in bed that morning, a text message from Terry came across her phone around 4:30, asking her to call him. She contemplated that a phone conversation this early in the morning couldn't yield good tidings. Instinctively, she felt it had to do with Jeremy, so she hesitated to make the call, fearing news that she wouldn't want to endure. Finally, she relented and called her cousin who uttered words that she never wished to hear from any parent—a child had died, Terry and Jill's son, her friend, and revered soldier. Kelly heard Terry speak these words but decided it must all be a bad dream. In desperation she called Leah for verification. Upon doing so, she could no longer deny the truth as dark devastation engulfed her. Her beloved cousin whom she adored and called her precious baby boy had perished.

While Kelly packed to go to Franklin, another cousin, Michael, called to check on her, resulting in one of the sweetest calls she ever received. On one of the most horrible days of her life, someone else put aside his pain and sincerely reached out to console and encourage her. She knew how close Jeremy and Michael were and how the news must have crushed him. She informed him of her impending trip to Franklin and that she would see him and his wife Kara there later that day. Finally packed, Kelly began the two-and-a-half-hour journey, which felt like a slow-motion odyssey. So many things raced through her mind, such as how she could have prevented this tragedy. With few details revealed at this juncture, Kelly repeatedly begged the question in her mind, *Why did this happen?* With so many unknowns swirling around in her head, she knew one thing for certain. She would never hug, hold hands, laugh, or cry with Jeremy again.

Pulling into the driveway, Kelly saw Leah standing about halfway to the garage. Upon parking, she walked straight to her, hugged her, and cried. Loss and sadness adorned Leah's countenance. Then Kelly saw Jill standing by the garage. No words availed to describe the suffering emanating from the woman who just lost her son. Speechless, the two ladies embraced in the midst of dim despair. Then Terry came out of the house to greet Kelly. A few years ago, he endured the anguish of losing his sister and now his son. Again, no words prevailed, just sorrow and tears. A short while later, Michael, Kara, and their daughter Briar pulled into the driveway.

Soon the little house bustled with people bringing food and with phones ringing off the hook, while under the ominous cloud of Jeremy's absence. Jill noticed one of Jeremy's favorite poems hanging on the side of the refrigerator. It now seemed to have a prophetic ring to it. The poem spoke of the trials and tribulations of a soldier's life. When the soldier stood before God to be judged, the Almighty declared that the soldier did his time in hell and bid him rest in heaven.

That afternoon the Smith family asked Kelly and Sharri to accompany them to the funeral home to make preparations. Kelly forced herself to go. Making funeral arrangements for a member of the younger generation seemed unnatural, out of order. Deep inside, she didn't want to do it. Nonetheless, she obliged them because they needed her support, and she would do anything for them at that juncture. They contemplated a burial plot for their revered soldier. Terry and Jill chose a location in the veterans' area of the cemetery just down the road from the funeral home. Jeremy's spot lay under a tree on a gentle hill where a nice breeze prevailed. This location pleased Kelly because it felt peaceful there. While a traumatic gale swirled within the soul of each, they completed all the other necessary business, taking comfort in the fact that they did it to honor Jeremy. Afterward, profound silence held them captive during the reticent drive home.

Upon their return to the Smith house, Cousin Timmy sat on the porch to greet them. Kelly joined Timmy there and proceeded to lay her heavy burden of grief upon him, which he gladly bore. For her, the rest of the evening seemed a blur. After everyone left, Kelly sat up with Terry as they cried, grieved, and ruminated over Jeremy. Any other time, they would laugh while revisiting some of his past antics. However, sorrow loomed too heavily upon them that evening. Sometime in the wee hours of the night, Kelly finally went to bed in Jeremy's room. This sleeping arrangement didn't bother her. On the contrary, it gave her much needed comfort. She even looked for the special purple bandana that bound the two of them together but couldn't find it. Jill eventually found it sometime later and presented it to Kelly, knowing that it held special meaning to her. Grateful, she now had a piece of Jeremy's heart to hold on to until she saw him again in heaven.

Saturday, August 4 presented a myriad of duties that nobody desired to fulfill. However, life demanded it, so the extended Smith family diligently worked away and managed to complete all necessary tasks of food preparation, receiving visitors, and making phone calls. That evening, Jeremy's old band played a tribute to him at the local Veterans of Foreign War (VFW) building. Many relatives, friends, and members of the community went to show their respect. As darkness fell at dusk, it paled in comparison to the darkness that befell the Smith family two days ago. Soon, tomorrow would present itself as another hard day of grieving and interacting with a multitude of people.

With sleep eluding them, the mournful family woke to Sunday morning. Kelly rejoiced to see her cousin and best friend Marianne pull into the driveway. Spending the time encouraging and comforting each other, it seemed that they had just walked into the house when the moment arrived to dress for the visitation ceremony that afternoon. Arriving at the funeral home for family time, they observed and mourned Jeremy before the ceremony opened to the community. Reality hit Leah like a ton of bricks as she gazed upon her brother in the casket for the first time. The surreal delusion evaporated as she could no longer pretend that this was all just a bad dream. The vast multitude of people who attended the ceremony comforted her. Looking back, Leah feared constantly that her brother would one day end all the pain, suffering, turmoil, and chaos of his life by suicide. She prayed for and cried over him every night. She honestly thought that his life would end a few years after his discharge from active duty. However, a tenacious warrior, Jeremy survived year after year, fighting to regain his life and to live the American dream for which he fought and suffered so deeply. He survived depression. He survived failed relationships. He survived disappointments. During much of 2018, he lived soberly and with optimism for the future, the former Jeremy slowly emerging.

Kelly recalled the heart-to-heart talks that she had with Jeremy over the years when he confided in her about his demons and about the importance of family. At the time, Kelly genuinely believed that her companionship and counsel helped him. Now that he died, she felt that she failed and could have done more. Never again will he come through the door of her house and give her one of his famous hugs that were the best in the world. Never again on this earth will his antics make them laugh until they could no longer breathe. When family time ended, Kelly walked to the kitchen area for a drink and observed an overwhelming sea of soldiers in the hallway and spilling outside the building into the parking lot. Soldiers came from all over the country, some having served with Jeremy fifteen years ago. Before the evening ended, even more arrived to say goodbye to their beloved fallen brother-in-arms. Kelly, along with other family members, stood in awe of the number of people who came to pay their respects that evening. She never saw so many grown men cry in her entire life. Yet, an even harder day loomed over the horizon with the dawning sun.

At the funeral the following day, Leah lovingly looked down upon her brother, caressing every feature of his stoic face. As the service progressed, so did her realization that this would be the last time that she would ever lay eyes on her older brother, her protector, her best friend. As they closed the casket, darkness closed in around her heart. This was it. Jeremy was gone for good. Two weeks later, she grieved heavily on his birthday. The following day, she received notice from her employer that her job had been eliminated. As the bread winner for her family, great angst pelted her as animosity toward God grew and flourished within her soul. She didn't understand why God allowed Jeremy to suffer all those years hoping for victory over his circumstances only to have his life snuffed out suddenly.

Almost a year later to the day, the anger and vitriol toward God evaporated from her soul as the hand of God delivered her from this turmoil when God met her where she was at spiritually. She finally accepted Jeremy's death and rededicated her life to God. She realized that Jeremy did get the victory because he now lived with God for all eternity. Looking back, Leah never questioned Jeremy's love for her. In that, she had the ultimate confidence. Additionally, his unfailing generosity for other people greatly impressed her.

♦♦♦

During the funeral, Kelly took comfort knowing that Jeremy finished his fight and that his physical, mental, and emotional pain ceased. Regardless, her heart broke in two when she entered and saw him in his custom-made suit lying in the wood casket, even though she had already seen him the previous night. Thankfully, Marianne and other family members provided comfort, while Kelly watched the legion of soldiers lined up with hearts torn out and tears of grief streaming as they left tokens of love in the casket with Jeremy. Pastor Herb Mays spoke the most heartfelt eulogy that she ever heard. Then Pastor Mays placed his token of love into Jeremy's casket, the suitcoat off his back symbolizing that he would do anything for him. These acts of love deeply touched and encouraged Kelly and her family. She knew for certain that Jeremy felt the same way, watching from above.

After the funeral ceremony, it seemed that everyone also went to the cemetery for the military burial with a twenty-one-gun salute. Of the hundreds there, not a dry eye prevailed as the soulful notes of Taps solemnly filled the air. Upon interment, Kelly left to start the rest of her life without her Smith boy. Life on this earth would never be the same for her with only his memory now living in her heart. With bittersweet tears rolling down her face, she felt grateful for the positive impact Jeremy had on her life.

Regardless, a piece of her soul would forever dwell down the road, atop a hill, under a soldier's headstone. In typical Jeremy fashion, however, everything he did blessed other people. From this experience, Kelly met some fine people she wouldn't have otherwise. She met Charlie Clabbers and had dinner at Aaron and Lauren Billings's home. She became friends with Jacob Mygatt, Eric Pollack, and Jordan Stransky. Bo White specifically touched her heart. She loved sharing stories of Jeremy's childhood with them. Jordan adopted Jeremy's dog Nubz. He brought Nubz when he and his family later visited Kelly. Nubz absolutely delighted her. These newfound friendships kept Jeremy alive for her. When thinking of him, she said in her heart, *I love you to the moon and around every planet and every star and back!*

♦♦♦

Back in the funeral parlor, Terry and Jill sat among family and friends. Jill missed her son tremendously but thanked God that she got to be his mom. She recalled what God said to her about giving Jeremy beauty for his ashes. The fulfillment of these words wasn't an earthly manifestation but a heavenly one. Jill recalled Isa 61:3 that read, "Giving them a garland instead of ashes, the oil of gladness instead of mourning, the cloak of praise instead of a disheartened spirit. So they will be called oaks of righteousness, the planting of the LORD, that He may be glorified." Jill took comfort in knowing that Jeremy no longer agonized. This lifted tremendous grief and worry off her shoulders. Hurting daily from the loss of her baby boy, she also looked forward to seeing him again in heaven. If she had the power to call him back to this world, she wouldn't do it knowing that he now lived in a better place.

She recalled how, for three days after he left for war, she couldn't control her crying or the heaviness of fear and grief that seized her. Jeremy's jacket hung in his bedroom closet. She clung to it daily and cried. It smelled like him. On the third day, she realized she wouldn't make it through this trial if she didn't get a grip. She grabbed her Bible and went to the porch to pray. She felt in her spirit the Lord say, "Jeremiah 31:16." She opened her Bible to that passage and read, "This is what the LORD says: 'Restrain your voice from weeping and your eyes from tears; for your work will be rewarded,' declares the LORD, 'and they will return from the land of the enemy.'" She knew at that moment of the importance of holding on to her faith. Jeremy's life depended on it. Subsequently, her Lord faithfully kept his promise to her. Jeremy returned home from the enemy's land three times. Greatest of all, God returned Jeremy to his heavenly home. This gave Jill hope for the future that she would see her son again just as soon as she went home as well.

Terry also greatly missed Jeremy. Just shy of thirty-five years old, his son departed this world, but it seemed that he shouldn't have. Despite this, Terry felt a subdued peace and joy knowing that his son no longer suffered. Gratitude in his heart toward God for Jeremy's salvation generated a calming warmth throughout Terry's being. Although decades may pass before Terry stepped into eternity, he felt that from Jeremy's perspective, it would seem only a few moments before they all reunited again. After the funeral, a butterfly often came to rest on the chair in the Smith family breezeway where Jeremy liked to sit. One frequently lit on Terry's knee as the family sat in the portico. They seemingly fluttered around everywhere after Jeremy passed, a tremendous comfort that still remained to this very day. Every time Jill saw a butterfly, she lovingly remembered that the Lord tarried with her son, as well as with her and the Smith family.

Terry and Jill also took great comfort in a letter that they received from Command Sergeant Major (CSM) (Retired) Brenda Kadet. She offered her deepest condolences over Jeremy's passing and emphasized how he significantly touched the lives of his fellow warriors. Other soldiers could always count on Jeremy whenever things got tough. As a pillar of strength and encouragement, he made them feel a degree safer in a world of combat. Although ten years had passed since they served together in Afghanistan, Jeremy loomed largely in her mind as one of the best.

Terry harbored no ill feelings toward the country or the Army for what his dad or his son suffered. Tragic things happened in war, which caused soldiers to carry pain and suffering in their hearts for a lifetime, the heavy price to pay for freedom and liberty. Soldiers could go to war and never get a physical scratch but come home deeply wounded within because the carnage profoundly impacted their psyche. Combat veterans more than likely left a part of their very soul on the battlefield and never really came home whole again. The emotional scars of combat stayed with these heroes for life. Most people in society might have an appreciation for what our veterans endured, but they didn't fully understand or know the depth of their sacrifice for our freedom and liberty. If that were the case, our combat veterans would receive better care.

Was the United States of America perfect? No. Could the government of this nation have done a better job caring for Jeremy? Yes. Be that as it may, the United States still hailed as the best country in the world offering unparalleled liberties and freedoms to its people. To Terry, Jill, Leah, and definitely Jeremy, the United States was well worth fighting for to preserve those blessings despite the unending offerings required upon the altar of freedom.

Resources Consulted

"562nd Engineer Company." U.S. Army Center of Military History. Accessed February 2019. https://history.army.mil/html/forcestruc/lineages/branches/eng/0562enco.htm.

"Afghanistan Climate." Afghanistan's Web Site. Accessed June 8, 2019. https://www.afghanistans.com/Information/Climate.htm.

"Afghanistan's Climate." The Swedish Committee for Afghanistan (SCA). Last modified May 22, 2018. https://swedishcommittee.org/afghanistan/climate.

"Anxiety and Intrusive Thoughts: An Introduction." Calm Clinic - Information About Anxiety, Stress & Panic. Accessed June 4, 2019. https://www.calmclinic.com/anxiety/signs/intrusive-thoughts.

"Army Sgt. Bryan C. Luckey| Military Times." Honor the Fallen | Military Times. Accessed July 11, 2019. https://thefallen.militarytimes.com/army-sgt-bryan-c-luckey/1927290.

"Army Sgt. Jeremiah J. Boehmer| Military Times." Honor the Fallen | Military Times. Accessed July 11, 2019. https://thefallen.militarytimes.com/army-sgt-jeremiah-j-boehmer/1521746.

"Army Staff Sgt. Christopher R. Morningstar| Military Times." Honor the Fallen | Military Times. Accessed July 11, 2019. https://thefallen.militarytimes.com/army-staff-sgt-christopher-r-morningstar/1521751.

"Climate and Average Weather in Iraq." World Weather & Climate Information. Accessed July 10, 2019. https://weather-and-climate.com/average-monthly-Rainfall-Temperature-Sunshine-in-Iraq.

"Combat! (TV Series)." Wikipedia, the Free Encyclopedia. Last modified January 26, 2002. https://en.m.wikipedia.org.

"Fairchild Republic A-10 Thunderbolt II." Wikipedia, the Free Encyclopedia. Last modified February 25, 2002. https://en.wikipedia.org/wiki/Fairchild_Republic_A-10_Thunderbolt_II.

"Franklin, KY Monthly Weather." The Weather Channel. Accessed February 2019. https://weather.com/weather/monthly/l/42134:4:US.

"Geography and Climate." Norwegian Afghanistan Committee. Accessed June 8, 2019. https://www.afghanistan.no/English/Afghanistan/Geography_and_climate/index.html.

"Geography of Afghanistan." Wikipedia, the Free Encyclopedia. Last modified November 6, 2001. https://en.wikipedia.org/wiki/Geography_of_Afghanistan.

"Gulf War." Wikipedia, the Free Encyclopedia. Last modified September 18, 2001. https://en.m.wikipedia.org/wiki/Gulf_War.

Hickman, Kennedy. "Iraq War: Second Battle of Fallujah." ThoughtCo. Last modified March 25, 2018. https://www.thoughtco.com/iraq-war-second-battle-of-fallujah-2360957.

"Hippocampus." Wikipedia, the Free Encyclopedia. Last modified May 28, 2002. https://en.wikipedia.org/wiki/Hippocampus.

"History of PTSD in Veterans: Civil War to DSM-5." VA.gov | Veterans Affairs. Accessed June 2, 2019. https://www.ptsd.va.gov/understand/what/history_ptsd.asp.

Holland, Kimberly. "Intrusive Thoughts: Why Everyone Has Them and How to Stop Them." Healthline. Accessed June 4, 2019. https://www.healthline.com/health/mental-health/intrusive-thoughts.

"Housing in Afghanistan and How Afghans Live." Transparent.com Blogs | Transparent Language. Last modified December 5, 2012. https://blogs.transparent.com/pashto/housing-in-afghanistan-and-how-afghans-live/.

"How Damage to the Brain's Hippocampus May Play a Role With PTSD." Verywell Mind. Accessed August 12, 2020. https://www.verywellmind.com/the-effect-of-ptsd-on-the-brain-2797643.

"How PTSD and Trauma Affect Your Brain Functioning." Psychology Today. Last modified September 29, 2018. https://www.psychologytoday.com/us/blog/the-mindful-self-express/201809/how-ptsd-and-trauma-affect-your-brain-functioning.

"International MaxxPro." Wikipedia, the Free Encyclopedia. Last modified June 1, 2007. https://en.wikipedia.org/wiki/International_MaxxPro.

"Intrusive Symptoms." Gracepoint. Accessed June 4, 2019. https://www.gracepointwellness.org/109-post-traumatic-stress-disorder/article/55732-intrusive-symptoms.

"Intrusive Thoughts & Memories." PTSD Trauma Treatment. Accessed June 5, 2019. https://www.ptsdtraumatreatment.org/intrusivethoughts/.

"Intrusive Thoughts and Post-Traumatic Stress Disorder (PTSD)." News-Medical.net. Last modified February 27, 2019. https://www.news-medical.net/health/Intrusive-Thoughts-and-Post-Traumatic-Stress-Disorder-(PTSD).aspx.

"Iraq War." Wikipedia, the Free Encyclopedia. Accessed March 2019. https://en.m.wikipedia.org/wiki/Iraq_War.

"Jessica Lynch." Wikipedia, the Free Encyclopedia. Accessed May 14, 2019. https://en.wikipedia.org/wiki/Jessica_Lynch.

Kime, Patricia. "Military Suicides Reach Highest Rate Since Record-Keeping Began After 9/11." Military.com. Last modified August 1, 2019. https://www.military.com/daily-news/2019/08/01/pentagon-reports-record-number-suicides.html.

Moore, Michael S. "PTSD Brain Studies Look at Hippocampus." Pacific Standard. Last modified July 6, 2011. https://psmag.com/news/ptsd-brain-studies-look-at-hippocampus-33419.

"Post-Traumatic Stress Disorder." NIMH » Home. Last modified May 2019. https://www.nimh.nih.gov/health/topics/post-traumatic-stress-disorder-ptsd/index.shtml.

"Post-traumatic Stress Disorder." Wikipedia, the Free Encyclopedia. Last modified September 9, 2002. https://en.wikipedia.org/wiki/Post-traumatic_stress_disorder.

"Posttraumatic Stress Disorder (PTSD)." WebMD. Last modified February 10, 2003. https://www.webmd.com/mental-health/post-traumatic-stress-disorder#1.

"Post-traumatic Stress Disorder (PTSD) - Symptoms and Causes." Mayo Clinic. Last modified July 6, 2018. https://www.mayoclinic.org/diseases-conditions/post-traumatic-stress-disorder/symptoms-causes/syc-20355967.

"PTSD." Make the Connection | Videos & Info for Military Veterans. Accessed June 4, 2019. https://maketheconnection.net/conditions/ptsd.

"PTSD in Military Veterans." HelpGuide.org. Accessed June 2, 2019. https://www.helpguide.org/articles/ptsd-trauma/ptsd-in-military-veterans.htm.

"PTSD in the Military: Statistics, Causes, Treatment, and More | Everyday Health." EverydayHealth.com. Last modified April 20, 2018. https://www.everydayhealth.com/ptsd/military-statistics-causes-treatment-more/.

"PTSD: National Center for PTSD Home." VA.gov / Veterans Affairs. Accessed June 2, 2019. https://www.ptsd.va.gov/understand/what/history_ptsd.asp.

"PTSD, the Hippocampus, and the Amygdala – How Trauma Changes the Brain." NICABM. Last modified July 14, 2020. https://www.nicabm.com/ptsd-the-hippocampus-and-the-amygdala-how-trauma-changes-the-brain/.

"Satellite Dandar Map — Share, Ruler, Find Your Location, Weather +forecast." ???? Satellite World Map — Share, Ruler, Find Your Location, Weather +forecast. Accessed June 12, 2019. https://satellites.pro/Dandar_map.Laghman_region.Afghanistan.

Shane, Leo, III. "New Veteran Suicide Numbers Raise Concerns Among Experts Hoping for Positive News." Military Times. Last modified October 9, 2019. https://www.militarytimes.com/news/pentagon-congress/2019/10/09/new-veteran-suicide-numbers-raise-concerns-among-experts-hoping-for-positive-news/.

Shiel, William C., Jr. "Definition of Labor." MedicineNet. Accessed February 2019. https://www.medicinenet.com/script/main/art.asp?articlekey=6194.

"Tagab District, Kapisa." Wikipedia, the Free Encyclopedia. Last modified May 3, 2007. https://en.wikipedia.org/wiki/Tagab_District,_Kapisa.

"Types of Delivery for Pregnancy." Cleveland Clinic. Last modified January 1, 2018. https://my.clevelandclinic.org/health/articles/9675-pregnancy-types-of-delivery.

"Understanding the Dangers of Alcohol Overdose." National Institute on Alcohol Abuse and Alcoholism (NIAAA). Last modified October 2018. https://www.niaaa.nih.gov/publications/brochures-and-fact-sheets/understanding-dangers-of-alcohol-overdose.

"Vehicle Checkpoints." *Defense Structures, Military Buildings, Blast & ForceProtection.* Accessed July 10, 2019. https://www.defence-structures.com/vehicle-checkpoints.html.

"Vietnam Statistics." US War Dog Association | National Headquarters. Accessed June 3, 2019. https://www.uswardogs.org/vietnam-statistics/.

"View Jeremy Doyle Smith's Obituary and Express Your Condolences." Legacy.com. Accessed February 2019. https://www.legacy.com/obituaries/name/jeremy-doyle-smith-obituary?pid=189801784.

Warden, James. "War Stories: Larger Than Life." Stars and Stripes. Last modified April 16, 2009. https://www.stripes.com/news/war-stories-larger-than-life-1.90358.

Wentling, Nikki. "VA Says Veteran Suicide Rate is 17 Per Day After Change in Calculation." Stars and Stripes. Last modified September 20, 2019. https://www.stripes.com/news/us/va-says-veteran-suicide-rate-is-17-per-day-after-change-in-calculation-1.599857.

"What Is PTSD?" Last modified January 2017. https://www.psychiatry.org/patients-families/ptsd/what-is-ptsd.

"Who Invented Ultrasound." CME Science. Accessed February 2019. https://cmescience.com/.

WireWerksTV. "Military Checkpoints." YouTube. Last modified November 15, 2006. https://www.youtube.com/watch?v=JK7wdtTpEGc.